THE
ANTHEM
SPRINTERS

And Other Antics

THE
ANTHEM
SPRINTERS

And Other Antics

by

Ray Bradbury

THE DIAL PRESS   NEW YORK   1963

Any resemblance between the characters herein and actual persons living or dead is purely coincidental.

NOTICE! No amateur or professional reading of this work may be given without permission in writing from the author's agent, Harold Matson Company, 30 Rockefeller Plaza, New York 20.

DESIGNED BY ALAN M. HEICKLEN

MANUFACTURED IN THE UNITED STATES OF AMERICA

BY THE COLONIAL PRESS INC., CLINTON, MASS.

To John Huston,
who sent me after the White Whale;

To Nick,
the cab-driver of Kilcock,
who helped me in my Search;

To Len and Beth Probst,
who found me when I was lost;

and to Maggie,
who brought me safely home.

CONTENTS

1. THE GREAT COLLISION OF MONDAY LAST   13
2. THE FIRST NIGHT OF LENT   41
3. A CLEAR VIEW OF AN IRISH MIST   69
4. THE ANTHEM SPRINTERS   123
5. THE QUEEN'S OWN EVADERS,
   An Afterword   149

THE
ANTHEM
SPRINTERS
And Other Antics

The Great Collision of
Monday Last

CHARACTERS

THE OLD MAN (MIKE)
THE YOUNG MAN (MC GUIRE)
HEEBER FINN
KELLY
FEENEY
QUINLAN
KILPATRICK
THE DOCTOR
PAT NOLAN
MR. PEEVEY
FLYNN
DONOVAN
CASEY

The curtain rises upon darkness. Later on, we will make out certain details, but now, in the dark, we hear someone whistling and singing, off away somewhere, an Irish ditty of some vintage or other; "Sweet Molly Malone" will do as well as any. The voice fades, then comes back, dies off into a kind of pumping gasp, and at last we see why, as onto the stage, wobbling badly, exhausted, pedals an old man on a bike. He more falls than gets off the damned thing in midstage and lets the beast lie there at his feet as he takes off his cap and wipes his brow, shaking his head.

The Old Man
Old Man, you're not what you once was!

He puts away his handkerchief, puts on his cap, bends to heft the bike, is still too winded and lets it fall.

Ah, lie there, brute that you are!

He takes out a bottle and eyes it sadly. There is but one last fiery gulp in it. He downs it philosophically and holds it up to let the last tiny drop fall off on his tongue. As he is doing so, we hear a car approach, stage left. Its lights flash out in a beam to spot THE OLD MAN, *who fends off the light with his free hand.*

Enough of that, now!

The lights go off, the motor cuts, a door opens and slams. THE YOUNG MAN *enters, stage left.*

The Young Man
Is anything wrong?

The Old Man (*blinking, peering*)
You made a blind man of me is all. Who's there? (*Squints*)

THE YOUNG MAN, *uncertain, takes half a step.*

13

THE YOUNG MAN

Oh, you don't know me—

THE OLD MAN

That's certain! (*Squints*) Is that an American voice I hear?

THE YOUNG MAN

I just got off the boat—

THE OLD MAN

He just got off the boat! He did indeed! Come closer!

THE YOUNG MAN *approaches*.

There! Me eyes are better. An American face to go with the American voice.

THE YOUNG MAN

May I be of assistance . . . ?

THE OLD MAN *holds the bottle up so it can drain its emptiness on the air*.

THE OLD MAN

Well, there's assistance *and* assistance. It came over me as I pumped up the hill, one or the other of us, me or this damned vehicle (*He kicks the bike gently*), is seventy years old.

THE YOUNG MAN

Congratulations.

THE OLD MAN

For what? Breathing? That's a habit, not a virtue.

THE YOUNG MAN

Let me give you a lift.

THE OLD MAN

No, a moment's rest, thanks, and me and the beast will be on our way. We don't know where we're going, Sally and me—

that's the damn bike's name—ye see, but we pick a road each day and give it a try.

THE YOUNG MAN, *who has been watchful and warming to this, now says, with real affection:*

THE YOUNG MAN
Does your mother know you're out?

THE OLD MAN (*surprised*)
Strange you say that! She does! Ninety-five she is, back there in the cot! Mother, I said, I'll be gone the day; leave the whisky alone!

He laughs to himself, quietly.

I never married, you know.

THE YOUNG MAN
I'm sorry.

THE OLD MAN
First you congratulate me for being old and now you're sorry I've no wife. It's sure you don't know Ireland. Being old and having no wives is one of our principal industries! You see, a man can't marry without property. You bide your time till your mother and father are called Beyond. Then when their property's yours, you look for a wife. It's a waiting game. I'll marry yet.

THE YOUNG MAN
At *seventy?*

THE OLD MAN (*ruffling*)
I'd get twenty good years out of marriage with a fine woman, even this late, do you doubt it!

THE YOUNG MAN (*impressed*)
I do not!

THE OLD MAN *relaxes.*

THE OLD MAN

Now, what are you up to, in Ireland?

THE YOUNG MAN

I'm looking for the Irish.

THE OLD MAN (*surprised, pleased, then mystified*)

Ah, that's difficult. They come, they throw shadows, they go.
You got one standing before you, now!

THE YOUNG MAN (*smiling*)

I know!

THE OLD MAN

You be a writer, of course.

THE YOUNG MAN

How did you guess!

THE OLD MAN (*gestures*)

The country's overrun! There's writers turning over rocks in
Cork and writers fishing in dinghies off Dun Laoghaire and
writers trudging through bogs at Kilashandra. The day will come,
mark me, when they will be five writers for every human being
in the world!

THE YOUNG MAN

Well, writer I am, and Irish I'm after. What shapes the Irish to
their dooms, and runs them on their way?

THE OLD MAN *eyes* THE YOUNG MAN *with not exactly suspicion,
but . . .*

THE OLD MAN

You're in the country two hours and already you sound like an
actor in the midst of the Abbey Theatre stage!

THE YOUNG MAN

Do I? Well, my family's all from Ireland, fifty years ago. So I
came to see their town, their land—their—

THE OLD MAN (*wincing*)
Enough! I got the sense of your jabber! Come here!

THE YOUNG MAN *steps closer.* THE OLD MAN *takes his shoulder.*

All right now, you say you want to bag the Irish in his lair? find him out? write him down? I'll take you to that place where you can spy on him unbeknownst! And where you'll see an event that's Irish as Irish can be—unseen before by outlander's eyes, or if seen not believed, or if believed not understood!

THE YOUNG MAN (*eagerly*)
An Event? a fair? a circus?

THE OLD MAN
A *sort* of circus, you might say . . . an unusual circumstance, the meeting of Fates is better! Hurry on, man, or we'll miss it!

THE OLD MAN *starts to trot, with his bicycle.*

THE YOUNG MAN
My car—

THE OLD MAN
Leave it there. It's not far.

TO MUSIC: THE YOUNG MAN *follows* THE OLD MAN *off into the wings, right. They reappear almost immediately, left,* THE OLD MAN *on the bike this time, pumping unsteadily along.*

THE OLD MAN (*pointing*)
Do you see those men there, walking on the road?

THE YOUNG MAN (*running behind*)
Yes!

THE OLD MAN
That's *not quite* the Irish!

TO MUSIC: *They vanish offstage right and reappear, left,* THE YOUNG MAN *still jogging after the old one on the bike.*

(*Pointing*) Do you see all them young fellows on their bikes pumping uphill?

THE YOUNG MAN (*breathless*)
Yes!

THE OLD MAN
That's *almost* the Irish.

TO MUSIC: *They vanish stage right, then reappear, left,* THE OLD MAN *seated on the crossbars of the bike,* THE YOUNG MAN *pumping.*

(*Pointing*) Do you see that sign, now?

THE YOUNG MAN (*gasping*)
Yes!

THE OLD MAN
Hold everything! *Stop!*

The bike wobbles and collapses. Both leap off barely in time. THE OLD MAN *points dramatically.*

That's the Irish!

A door has slid out of the wings, right. A sign has come down out of the flies. THE YOUNG MAN *reads it aloud.*

THE YOUNG MAN
Heeber Finn's. (*His face takes fire*) Why . . . it's a *pub!*

THE OLD MAN (*all innocence*)
By God, now, I think you're right! (*He runs to the pub door*) Come meet my family!

THE YOUNG MAN
Family? You said you weren't married!

THE OLD MAN

I'm not! But a man, seventy or no, has got to have a family. Right? Well!

THE OLD MAN *rams the double wicket doors, plunges through. At this instant the scrim goes from front to back lighting. Instantaneously we see the inside of Heeber Finn's pub, the men at the bar, and Finn himself working the spigots. Once the lighting is established, the scrim can go up out of the way.*

At the sound of the doors flung back, the men at the bar jerk.

It's *me,* boys!

HEEBER FINN, *behind the bar, sighs.*

FINN

Mike! **Ya gave us a start!**

ANOTHER MAN

We thought it was—a *crisis!*

THE OLD MAN *is pleased with the savor of that word.*

THE OLD MAN

Well, maybe it is! This is my friend!

He points to THE YOUNG MAN. *Now he points to the others.*

. . . and these, you might say, are what I use for a family . . .

THE YOUNG MAN *is touched by this fancy, and nods to all. The men murmur in friendly fashion, nodding.*

FINN

Has your friend a crisis, then, Mike?

THE OLD MAN *sobers dramatically.*

THE OLD MAN

He's come to see the Irish, clear!

FINN *pours from a bottle.*

> ### FINN
> See it or drink it?

> ### THE YOUNG MAN
> A—bit of both.

> ### FINN
> Well spoke. To your health.

He shoves the glass across the counter, winking. THE OLD MAN *leans, peering, toward the door.*

> ### THE OLD MAN
> Fine! it's dark early. Ah, that lovely mist! Now, peel an eye, Young Man. There's great events preparing themselves out in that fog, of all kinds and sorts even *I* can't tell you; right, boys?

The men assent. THE YOUNG MAN *drinks, gasps.*

> ### THE YOUNG MAN (*peering*)
> What should I look for?

> ### THE OLD MAN
> Let nothing pass unquestioned! (*Turns*) Give 'em another, Finn, to focus his eyes.

FINN *pours.* THE YOUNG MAN *wisely lets it lie.* THE OLD MAN *trots to the door, half opening same to let in a wisp of fog, which he fingers.*

Will you look? Why, you could wear the dainty stuff about your neck! A fine night. *Anything* could happen! and always *does!*

He inhales the fog, the lovely dark, smiles at the aroma, lets the doors shimmy shut, and comes back to the bar to sip his drink.

Mind, now, maybe you'll have to wait for some other night—

FINN (*incensed*)

Can you name one night in history wasn't a night of earth-shaking consequence at Heeber Finn's?

THE OLD MAN (*scratches head*)

I can't.

FINN

You can't. (*Turns*) Son, do you play darts?

THE YOUNG MAN

Yes.

FINN

Good! Do you lie?

THE YOUNG MAN

Lie?

FINN

Can you tell untruths, man? Big ones, small, all sizes?

THE YOUNG MAN (*dubiously*)

I'll try.

FINN (*pleased*)

I'm sure you will! We——

Suddenly THE OLD MAN *quickens, catching hold of elbows to right and left.*

THE OLD MAN

Hist!

All down the bar, everyone freezes.

(*Whispering*) That was *it!*

Every head, on a single string, turns toward the door.

THE YOUNG MAN

What . . . ?

THE OLD MAN

Ssst! *Listen* . . .

All lean. All hear—something, far away.

(*Eyes shut*) That's it . . . yes . . . yes . . .

Everyone stares. Footsteps batter the outside step drunkenly. The double wing doors flap wide as a bloody man in his thirties staggers in, capless, holding his bloody head with a bloody hand. He stops, blinking numbly at the crowd.

THE YOUNG MAN *stares, amazed.*

All down the bar, the men lean toward the intruder.

The intruder sways, trying to find words, eyes glazed.

THE OLD MAN *moves forward, frantically curious, gesturing his hand as if bidding the man to speak up, speak up!*

The bloody intruder finally gasps for breath.

THE INTRUDER

Collision! Collision on the road!

Then, chopped at the knees, he falls down. The men glance at each other.

ALL

Collision!

HEEBER FINN *vaults the bar. His landing breaks the spell.*

FINN

Kelly, Feeney, quick!

All run toward the "body." HEEBER FINN *is first, with* THE OLD MAN.

THE OLD MAN

Easy does it!

FINN

Quinlan, out to the road! Mind the victim! Kilpatrick, run for the Doc!

A Voice

Wait!

ALL *look up.*

THE DOC *steps out from the far end of the bar, from a little dark cubby where he has been standing alone with his philosophies.*

FINN *is surprised.*

FINN

Doc, you're so quiet I forgot you was there! Out you go!

THE DOCTOR *plunges out the front door with half a dozen men. The fog streams in past them.*

THE YOUNG MAN *looks down at the "victim" on the floor. The "victim's" lips twitch.*

THE VICTIM (*gasping, whispering*)

Collision . . .

FINN

Softly, boys.

They lift "the victim" and carry him over to lay him on the bar.

THE YOUNG MAN *comes up to stare at the man lying there, and at his image in the mirror behind the bar . . . two dread calamities for the price of one.*

THE YOUNG MAN (*puzzled*)

But . . . I didn't hear any cars on the road.

THE OLD MAN *is proud to reply:*

THE OLD MAN

That you didn't!

He beckons. With a high sense of melodrama, THE OLD MAN *escorts him to the swinging doors, opens one for him.*

A scrim has come down as they move toward the door.

As they emerge into the "outside," the "world," the lights go off behind the scrim and come on in front of it. This particular

*scrim is a mist, a fog, a gray background across which they may
wander, looking out over the apron at the night, the weather,
and the men foraging beyond. There are wisps of fog or mist
moving in from either side, from the wings, and from below in
the pit.*

THE OLD MAN *stands next to the young one, on the steps of
the pub, sniffing the weather appreciatively.*

You'd almost think that Ireland was gone. Oh, but it's there,
all right.

THE YOUNG MAN *stares into the fog, continuing his thought.*

THE YOUNG MAN
. . . nor did I hear a collision.

THE OLD MAN (*shouting beyond*)
Try the crossroad, boys! That's where it most often does!
(*Quieter, he turns to* THE YOUNG MAN) Ah, we don't be great
ones for commotion, nor great crashing sounds. But collision
you'll see if you step on out there. (*Points stage left*)

THE YOUNG MAN *moves stage left, probing into the fog, groping.*

Walk now, don't run! It's the Devil's own night. You might
head-on into Feeney, too drunk to find any road, no matter
what's on it. You got a match?

THE YOUNG MAN
A match?

THE OLD MAN
Blind you'll be, but try it!

THE YOUNG MAN *strikes a match, holds it out in front of him.*

That's pitiful poor, but on you go, and me behind you. Careful
now, *walk!*

Both move in a great circle about the stage.

Hist, now!

They listen to a rally of voices approaching.

Here they come!

> A VOICE (*hidden in fog*)
Easy now. Don't jiggle him!

> ANOTHER VOICE
Ah, the shameful blight!

Suddenly from the fog, stage left, a steaming lump of men appear bearing atop themselves a crumpled object.
THE YOUNG MAN *stares up, holding the match. We glimpse a bloodstained and livid face high up there.*
Someone brushes the lit match, which snuffs out.
The catafalque rushes on.

> A VOICE
Where's Heeber Finn's?

> ANOTHER VOICE
Bear left, left, I say!

The crowd vanishes. THE YOUNG MAN *peers after. He hears a chilling insect rattle approach in the fog. He strikes another match.*

> THE YOUNG MAN
Who's there?

> A VOICE
It's us!

> ANOTHER VOICE
With the vehicles!

THE YOUNG MAN *blinks at the old, who nods sagely.*

> A VOICE
You might say we got—the collision!

Two men trot out of the fog, bringing with them under their arms two ancient black bicycles, minus head and taillights.

THE YOUNG MAN *stares at them. The two men with the bikes smile, proud of their task, give the bikes a heft, tip their caps, and trot off away again, vanishing in mist, toward Finn's, just as the last match dies forever.* THE YOUNG MAN, *stunned with the simple facts, hangs his mouth open, turning to* THE OLD MAN.

THE YOUNG MAN

What?

THE OLD MAN (*winks*)

What? What, indeed! Ah, the delightful mysteries!

And he runs off into fog. THE YOUNG MAN, *musing, follows.*

THE YOUNG MAN

Men . . . *bicycles* . . . collision? Old Man, wait for *me!*

THE YOUNG MAN *runs, finds the front door to Finn's, and plunges in. The lights come on inside Finn's, the fog-scrim vanishes.*

   Inside Finn's, THE OLD MAN *turns to welcome the arrival of* THE YOUNG MAN.

THE OLD MAN

Ah, there you are! (*lowers voice to a whisper*) We got the "bodies" on the bar.

THE YOUNG MAN *peers over the crowd at the two "bodies" laid out in pale ruin on the long bar,* THE DOC *moving fretfully between the two, shouldering the crowd aside.*

   THE OLD MAN *whispers:*

One's Pat Nolan. Not under employment at the moment.

THE OLD MAN *peers and nods at the next.*

The other's Mr. Peevey from Meynooth. In candy and cigarettes, mostly.

THE OLD MAN *raises his voice.*

Are they long for this world, now, Doc?

THE DOC *mutters, swabbing a marbled face.*

> ### THE DOC
Ah, be still, won't ya! Here, let's put one victim on the floor.

THE DOC *moves.* FINN *stops him.*

> ### FINN
The floor's a tomb. He'll catch his death down there. Best leave him up where the warm air gathers from our talk.

THE DOC *shrugs and continues working.* THE YOUNG MAN *whispers in* THE OLD MAN'*s hairy ear.*

> ### THE YOUNG MAN
But I've never heard of an accident like this in all my life!

> ### THE OLD MAN (*fascinated with* THE DOC)
That you didn't!

> ### THE YOUNG MAN
Are you sure there were absolutely no cars?

> ### THE OLD MAN
None.

> ### THE YOUNG MAN
Only these two men on their bikes?

> ### THE OLD MAN (*turning*)
Only! *Only!*

> ### THE YOUNG MAN (*embarrassed*)
I mean—

> ### THE OLD MAN
Great gods, man, what do you *know* of buy-cycles?

> ### THE YOUNG MAN
Just—

> ### THE OLD MAN
Just nothing! Clear the way!

THE OLD MAN *fists a path to the two bikes leaned to the wall.*

Flynn! Donovan! Lend a hand! Casey, the other bike!

He kicks the backstand of the bike down. He swings astride a bike. The men grab front and back to steady it. CASEY *does likewise with the second bike.*

Where am I now?

THE YOUNG MAN

In Heeber Finn's—

THE OLD MAN

No! I'm on the Meynooth Road . . . idling home lazy as you please . . .

He pumps. The back wheel, being free, hums quietly at a nice easy pace. CASEY *pumps, too.*

(*Listens*) I hear a church bell. I know I'm late for meals. So what do I do?

THE YOUNG MAN (*trying*)

Go faster?

THE OLD MAN

Now you're with it, lad! Faster I go! Where before I was toddling along easy at twenty or twenty-five, now here I work up a drizzling sweat at—

FLYNN

Forty an hour!

THE OLD MAN

Forty-five! Fifty!

He pumps furiously, bent down in concentrated passion.

Now with a long downhill glide I hit sixty! So here I come, with no front or taillights.

THE YOUNG MAN

Isn't there a law against that?

THE OLD MAN

To hell with government interference! So here I come!

CASEY

And here *I* come! the other way!

Both pump furiously, heads down.

THE OLD MAN

The two of us, no lights, heads down, flying home from one town to the next, thrashing like Sin himself's at our behinds! Both going opposite ways—

CASEY

But both on the *same side* of the road!

THE OLD MAN

Always ride the wrong side of the road, lad, it's safer, they say! But look on those boys, fair destroyed by all that official palaver. Why? One remembered it, the other didn't! Better if the officials kept their mouths shut! For there the two boys lie, dying!

THE YOUNG MAN *stares. The wheels hum, whining!*

THE YOUNG MAN

Dying?

CASEY (*pumping*)

Well, think on it, man! What stands between two able-bodied hell-bent fellas jumping along the path from Kilcock to Meynooth?

THE OLD MAN (*pumping*)

Fog! Fog is all. Only fog to keep their skulls from bashing together. So look now! Here we come, *bang!*
The old man jerks his bike up in the air with a grand whining, humming flourish, as does CASEY.

There we go, nine feet up in the air, heads together like dear chums met, flailing the mist, our bikes clenched like two tomcats. Then we all fall down and just lay there, feeling around for the Dark Angel.

*They let the bikes fall and stand over them, looking down at the
imaginary wreckage.*

THE YOUNG MAN *looks from them to the bar.*

THE YOUNG MAN
Surely these men won't—

CASEY
Oh, *won't* they? Why, last year alone in all the Free State, no
night passed some soul did not meet in fatal collision with another.

THE YOUNG MAN (*aghast*)
You mean to say over three hundred Irish bicyclists die every
year, hitting each other?

THE OLD MAN *bows his head as at the grave of a friend.*

THE OLD MAN
God's truth and a pity!

HEEBER FINN *eyes the "bodies."*

FINN
I never ride my bike nights. I *walk*.

THE YOUNG MAN
Why . . . let's get them to a hospital, then, quick!

THE OLD MAN *is mildly irritated at this interruption of their
round-robin discussion.*

THE OLD MAN
One thing at a time, please. You was saying, Finn . . . ?

FINN
I walk!

CASEY
But even walking, the damn bikes run you down!

THE OLD MAN
True!

CASEY

Awheel, or afoot, some idiot's always pantin' up doom the other way, they'd sooner split you down the seam than wave hello!

THE YOUNG MAN (*touching* THE OLD MAN'S *elbow*)
The victims here—

THE OLD MAN

One moment, lad. (*Shakes head*) Ah, the brave men I've seen ruined or half-ruined or worse, and headaches their lifetimes after.

He looks at the bicycles on the floor between them, and trembles, his eyelids shut.

You might almost think, mightn't you, that human beings was not made to handle such delicate instruments of power.

THE YOUNG MAN (*still dazed*)
Three hundred dead each year . . .

CASEY

And that don't count the "walkin' wounded" by the thousands every fortnight who, cursing, throw their bikes in the bog forever and take government pensions to salve their all-but-murdered bodies.

THE YOUNG MAN (*nervously*)
I hate to bring it up but should we stand here just *talking?*

THE OLD MAN (*wounded, as are the others*)
Just talking! We're debating the problems and making the decisions! Look there, do ya see?

They look.

THE DOC, *quite obviously enjoying his moment of power in center stage of the crowd, walks back and forth between the two creatures on the bar. The crowd looks after him from right to left. He is building his moment of suspense. He squints one eye, closes both, rubs his chin, scratches his ear.*

THE MEN (*restlessly*)

Ah . . .

THE DOC *realizing he has gone almost too far, feeling his audience begin to drift away, now snatches their attention back by straightening up and exhaling briskly.*

THE DOC

Well, now!

The men quicken.

THE OLD MAN *whispers to* THE YOUNG MAN, *grabbing his arm.*

THE OLD MAN

He's ready for his pronouncement!

THE DOC, *veteran of much medical play-acting, rocks on his feet, and points at the first "body."*

THE DOC

This chap here—

The crowd leans toward the chap.

Bruises, lacerations, and agonizin' backaches for two weeks runnin'.

Everyone nods at the shame of it. THE DOC *now turns to the other and makes his face grim. The men lean that way.*

As for this one—

He pauses.

(*In a dramatic whisper*) Concussion.

ALL

Concussion!

The quiet wind of their voices rises and falls in the silence.

THE DOC

He'll survive if we run him quick now to Meynooth Clinic. Now then—whose car will volunteer?

The crowd looks at itself, then turns as a staring body toward
THE YOUNG MAN. *He feels the gentle shift as he is drawn from*
outside the ritual to its deep and innermost core. He looks about,
thinking perhaps there may be another volunteer. Then he walks
to the door, half opens it, and looks out.

THE YOUNG MAN (*counting*)
. . . twelve . . . fourteen . . . sixteen bicycles . . . and, two
hundred yards down the road . . . one automobile . . . *mine.*

THE OLD MAN
Praise God, that's fortunate!

THE YOUNG MAN *turns sheepishly. The crowd leans toward him.*
THE YOUNG MAN *nods, once.* THE DOC *quickens with gratitude.*

THE DOC
A volunteer!! Quick, lads, now, hustle this victim—gently—to
our good friend's vehicle. Take his keys. Drive the car up outside!

THE YOUNG MAN *holds out the keys as someone runs by, seizing*
them. The men reach out to lift the body and freeze when THE
YOUNG MAN *clears his throat. All look to him.* THE YOUNG MAN
circles them with his hand, tips his cupped hand to his mouth,
and nods at FINN. *The men gasp.*

CASEY
He's right, of course! It's a cold night. One for the road!

HEEBER FINN *lines up the shot glasses lip to lip and sprinkles*
them all quickly with the passing bottle. Hands seize the glasses.
One of the victims is taken off the bar and set in a chair, where,
reviving, his face like a white cheese, he feels a glass put in his
trembly hand.

THE OLD MAN
Here, lad, now . . . tell us . . .

CASEY

What happened, eh . . . ? eh?

*The drinks are gulped. The second victim is hefted. The men
head for the door.* THE YOUNG MAN, *amazed, watches them go,
his drink in his hand.*

THE OLD MAN

Finish your drink, Mr. . . . ?

THE YOUNG MAN (*faintly*)

McGuire.

THE OLD MAN

By the saints, he *is* Irish!

THE YOUNG MAN *looks—at the recovering victim, at the bar, the
mirrors, the two bikes against the wall, the fog seeping in through
the door, then, at last, at* THE OLD MAN, *and the depths of the
drink in his hand.*

THE YOUNG MAN (*thoughtfully*)

No . . . I don't think I am.

He swigs his drink and heads for the door with THE OLD MAN
*dogtrotting after. At the door he stops, for a voice is speaking
behind him. He does not turn, but listens. Behind, over his
shoulder, the recovered "victim" is sipping his drink and talking
to two men bent earnestly to listen.*

THE VICTIM (*hoarsely, dramatically*)

Well . . . I'm on me way home, blithe as you please, see, and—

THE YOUNG MAN *steps through the doors quickly. The pub lights
go out. Outside, the fog-scrim appears, mist drifts in from either
side. We hear voices off and away, and the approach of* THE
YOUNG MAN's *car, driven by someone. The car stops, just out of
sight.*

A VOICE

There we are!

ANOTHER VOICE

Now, easy, inside with the poor victim!

THE YOUNG MAN *muses, with* THE OLD MAN *beside him, in the night.*

THE YOUNG MAN

Old Man, do you ever have auto wrecks, collisions between people in *cars?*

THE OLD MAN (*insulted*)

Not in our town!! If you like *that* sort of thing, now (*Nods scornfully east*), Dublin's the very place for it!

THE YOUNG MAN *looks east, nods, moves toward his car offstage.*

Look now, McGuire, a last bit of advice. You've driven little in Ireland, right?

THE YOUNG MAN *nods.*

Listen. Driving to Meynooth, fog and all, go fast! Raise a din!

THE YOUNG MAN

In this fog? Why?

THE OLD MAN

Why, he asks! To scare the bicyclists off the path, *and* the cows! Both sides! If you drive slow, you'll creep up on and do away with dozens before they know what took them off. Also—when another car approaches—douse your lights, pass each other, lights out, in safety. Them devil's own lights have put out more eyes and demolished more innocents than all of seeing's worth. Is it clear, now?

THE YOUNG MAN *nods.*

You got a cap? I see ya haven't. So—

THE OLD MAN *produces a tweed cap from his coat pocket.*

THE OLD MAN

Put this on! Bicycling, driving, or especially, walking, *always* wear

a cap. It'll save you the frightful migraines should you meet
Kelly or Moran or some other hurtling full tilt the other way,
full of fiery moss and hard-skulled from birth! So you see, there's
rules for pedestrians, too, in our country, and *wear a cap,* is
Number One!

THE YOUNG MAN *pulls the cap down and looks to* THE OLD MAN
for his approval, which he gets.

THE OLD MAN
Well now, get along, lad.

THE YOUNG MAN
Aren't you riding with me?

THE OLD MAN
Ah, no, I got the beast here, I must check on the mother.

*He picks up his bike and slings a slatty leg over it and pulls his
cap down.*

THE OLD MAN
Well, sir, did you find what you came for? did you see the Irish,
clear?

THE YOUNG MAN
I saw but didn't see . . . lost one thing and found another . . .
now, *that's* gone, too. Tell me, how did you guess all this would
happen tonight, here? How did you know?

THE OLD MAN
I didn't! Some other night it would be some other thing! Like
I said, anything could happen, and always does! That's Ireland
for you. And it's waiting out there for you now, in the fog. Go
find it!

THE YOUNG MAN *runs off, stage right.*

THE YOUNG MAN
I will!

We hear the motor revved, offstage.

THE OLD MAN (*shouting off*)
Remember what I said! Douse your lights!

The lights go off, stage right.

THE OLD MAN (*shouting*)
Go fast!

Offstage, we hear the furious gunning of the motor.

THE OLD MAN
Keep your cap on! Tight! (*Yanks his own cap, hard*)

THE YOUNG MAN (*offstage*)
See you again!

THE OLD MAN
God willing!

We hear the car roar off and away. The sound fades.
When it is gone, THE OLD MAN is alone on his bike. He prepares
himself, clears his throat, and sings going off, stage right.

THE OLD MAN
"She wheeled her wheelbarrow . . ."

At which moment, a shadowy bicyclist (FINN) comes through
the other way. They almost collide.

THE OLD MAN
Damn! Watch where you're going!

FINN
Hell! Look what you're doing!

THE OLD MAN
Heeber Finn, it's you!

FINN
Old man, it's you!

THE OLD MAN

God Bless!

FINN

God Bless! (*Takes up the song, sailing away*)
"She wheeled her wheelbarrow. . ."

THE OLD MAN (*sings*)
". . . through streets wide and narrow . . ."

They vanish, pumping, but to reappear, wave, pass, and go off in darkness, alternating lines of song, vanishing at last as the mist and dark take over:

HEEBER FINN
". . . singing cockles . . ."

THE OLD MAN
". . . and mussels . . ."

HEEBER FINN
". . . alive! . . ."

THE OLD MAN
". . . alive! . . ."

BOTH TOGETHER
". . . Ohhhh! . . ."

By this time the curtain has hushed down on the mist and the play is at. . .

THE END

The First Night of Lent

CHARACTERS

THE YOUNG MAN (DOUGLAS)

MIKE (THE OLD MAN)

HEEBER FINN

TIMULTY

NOLAN

O'CONNELL

PURDY

KELLEEN

SEAN (TELEPHONE OPERATOR)

Curtain up on darkness.

THE YOUNG MAN *strolls along in the dark to a single spotlight where he stands debating with himself, hands in pockets, head down.*

Off somewhere, a harp begins to play a few bars of "Mollie Malone" or some such ditty.

THE YOUNG MAN *raises his hands.*

THE YOUNG MAN

Please. No harp. That will only muddy the waters and stop us from thinking clear about Ireland.

The harp rushes to the end of the next few bars, as if to get it all in, then ceases. THE YOUNG MAN *nods, not surprised at this maneuver, and continues, looking out at the audience.*

Does anyone understand the Irish?
No.
Will anyone *ever* understand them in all of time?
No.
Can there be some system or method to size and sort them, tincture their ganglions so we can slide them under a microscope and see what makes them dance? (*Shakes his head*)
No history can date them, no psychiatrist's couch lure them, no song explain them. And yet, as others tried, now so must I.
Did I ever know one solitary Irish fellow well?
I did. His name? Mike.

MIKE *sticks his head out of the wings, left.*

MIKE

Ya called, sir?

THE YOUNG MAN

In a moment, Mike—

41

MIKE

Take all the time in the world!

MIKE's *head vanishes.*

THE YOUNG MAN

I knew Mike for two hundred consecutive nights—

MIKE'S VOICE (*offstage*)

Two-hundred-*one!*

THE YOUNG MAN

—two-hundred-one consecutive nights of one fall, winter, and early spring when I went to Ireland to write a film. I lived in Dublin, and every day when I finished ten new fresh pages of script, I would hire a taxi out to Kilcock, show my director my work, and at midnight go back to Dublin. How? By hiring the only taxi for miles around. So, every night I'd call the village exchange.

He picks up a telephone. And perhaps to one side, now, spotlighted, we can see SEAN, THE TELEPHONE OPERATOR, *bent over the village switchboard.*

SEAN

Are ya there?

THE YOUNG MAN

Hello, would you—

SEAN

Ah, it's *you,* Mr. Douglas.

THE YOUNG MAN

Who's this?

SEAN

Why, Sean, of course!

THE YOUNG MAN

Sean?

SEAN

The wife's got the uneasies. I took over the village *ex*-change for tonight.

THE YOUNG MAN

Good . . .

SEAN

A fine night.

THE YOUNG MAN

It is.

SEAN

It must be up to at least fifty degrees on the damn thermometer.

THE YOUNG MAN

All of that.

SEAN

Warm for this time of year.

THE YOUNG MAN

I always said, Dublin is the Riviera of Ireland.

SEAN

Did ya, now? I must remember to tell the wife. I suppose Heeber Finn's is where you're calling?

THE YOUNG MAN

If you don't mind, Sean.

SEAN

Mind! I'll put ya through like a bolt of lightning!

There is a hissing crackle. From the phone now pours a veritable millrace of voices, laughter, tinkling bottles, toasts, brags, and general multitude of hilarity. In the background, through a scrim, we see Finn's, and the crowd there at the bar. THE YOUNG MAN *listens, fascinated.*

(*At last*) I have reason to believe you are through to Heeber Finn's, sir.

THE YOUNG MAN (*listening*)

I don't doubt it, Sean.

We see FINN, *behind the bar, maneuvering drinks and the phone.*

FINN'S VOICE (*shouting*)

Heeber Finn here! Who's on the other end!

SEAN

Heeber, it's *himself* from the big house!

THE YOUNG MAN *starts to speak but is cut across.*

FINN

Mr. Douglas, is it?

SEAN

The same!

FINN

Always glad to hear from Mr. Douglas.

THE YOUNG MAN *starts to speak, but—*

SEAN

Did you know he was a writer?

FINN (*awed*)

I *did* not!

THE YOUNG MAN *opens his mouth, nodding.*

SEAN

He is! Writes them science and fiction stories!

FINN (*dismayed*)

How's that?

SEAN

You know; them shiny magazines with the green monsters chasing raw naked women over the Martian Hills on the covers!

FINN (*pleased*)

So *that's* what he's up to!

THE YOUNG MAN *opens his mouth, but—*

SEAN

He is also writing the fillum with the title *Moby Dick.*

FINN

Is he?

THE YOUNG MAN *nods, defeated. He does not try to open his mouth any more.*

SEAN

You know the story, about the Whale!

FINN

And Jonah in his belly!

THE YOUNG MAN

No—

SEAN

No, man. Ahab!

FINN

What?

THE YOUNG MAN (*getting it in fast*)

Ahab!

FINN

Who else is on the line, Sean?

SEAN

Himself!

FINN

Ahab?

SEAN

Mr. Douglas, ya dimwit!

FINN

Hello, **Mr. Douglas!**

THE YOUNG MAN

I——

FINN

Now, who's this Ahab?

SEAN

Ahab is the captain that hunts the White Whale, man!

FINN

A fine story. Are ya there, Mr. Douglas? I said . . .

THE YOUNG MAN

Mr. Finn. Could you find Mike, the taxi driver, for me?

FINN

He's good as found.

There is a long silence. We watch and hear the mob at Finn's and FINN *himself calling off and away:* "Mike, Mike!"

SEAN

It's a fine night, Mr. Douglas.

THE YOUNG MAN (*by rote*)

A bit warm for this time of year.

SEAN (*admiring the other's sense*)

Just what *I* was thinking——!

We see a man jog through the crowd, rear, and grab the phone.

ANOTHER VOICE (*breaking in*)

Hello, Mr. Douglas?

THE YOUNG MAN

Mike?

ANOTHER VOICE

No. He'll be here when he finishes his game of darts!

We see MIKE, *rear, playing the game out.*

THE YOUNG MAN

Never mind, just tell Mike—

We see MIKE *forging toward the phone.*

ANOTHER VOICE

Hold on, here comes the triumphant victor now!

THE YOUNG MAN

There's no—

MIKE'S VOICE

Mr. Douglas, congratulate me!

THE YOUNG MAN

Mike, is that you?

MIKE'S VOICE

Who else? And I won!

THE YOUNG MAN

Mike, can you drive me to Dublin, now?

MIKE

I'm halfway to the door!

There is a thud as, presumably, the phone is dropped at the other end. The crowd noises swell. THE YOUNG MAN *holds the receiver off and looks at it with bemusement, then addresses the audience again.*

THE YOUNG MAN

Halfway to the door. It is but thirty feet, I'd wager, from the bar of Heeber Finn's to the far side of the pub where the door, neglected, abhorrent, waits. Yet that thirty feet is best negotiated carefully, and may take all of one minute per foot. In other words, it may take Mike half an hour to go from the phone to the outside world and five minutes to drive the half-mile up the road to where I am waiting for him. Listen to them.

He holds out the phone, taking his hand off the earpiece so the noise swells.

Mike's on his way. He's halfway to the door, plus one foot.

And this is true. During all the above, in dim pantomime behind the rear scrim, we see MIKE *turning in slow circles, moving his head here, there, touching this person, touching that, trying to finish a stout thrust in his hand, answering a jest with another, laughing at one man, scowling at a second, blinking at a third. The pantomime continues during the following speech.*

Do you see how patient I am? Do I yell or threaten? I do not. I learned, early on, that Mike's "headin' for the door" was no nerve-shattering process for him. He must not affront the dignity of the men he moves among. He must admire, on his way out, the fine filigree of any argument being woven with great and breathless beauty at his elbow or behind his back. It is, for him, a gradual disengagement, a leaning of his bulk so his gravity is diplomatically shifted toward that far empty side of the public room where the door, shunned by all, stands neglected. On his way, a dozen conversational warps and woofs must be ticked, tied, and labeled so next morn, with hoarse cries of recognition, patterns may be seized, the shuttle thrown with no pause or hesitation.

THE YOUNG MAN *produces a long instructor's pointer or baton.*

To give you an idea of Mike's debilitating journey across the pub, here, for instance—

He points to one of the men who, approached by MIKE *now, breaks into a kind of jig or reel.*

That's old Timulty, who will dance for any reason or no reason at all.

MIKE *is appreciative of the jig and perhaps joins in a once-around.*

THE YOUNG MAN *points to a second man ahead.*

Here's Pat Nolan. A fierce outcaster of politics. A banger, a smasher and a shouter, to the wonderment of all.

Now that TIMULTY *has been gotten by,* MIKE *is confronted by* NOLAN, *who has two other men by their ties or lapels—that is, when he is not banging his own knee or smashing his fist into one palm. Now, as* MIKE *happens along,* NOLAN *sees him and, in pantomime, grabs out for him and starts bellowing on some vasty argument or other.* MIKE *is totally impressed, and nods, nods, nods.*

THE YOUNG MAN *points farther on—one, two, three.*

While up ahead waits O'Connell with his jokes.

We see O'CONNELL *laughing at his own stories, holding to some-one's shoulder.*

Purdy with his harmonica.

PURDY *is guzzling his harmonica as we see him swaying there.*

And Kelleen with a brand-spanking-new poem he is just finishing . . .

We see KELLEEN, *using someone's back for a desk, scribbling furiously on a crumpled paper.*

There! Mike's almost to the door. He's got the doorknob in his hand!

Which is true. We see it!

Now, he—

At this instant, far across the pub, on the other side, a man waves and shouts in pantomime. MIKE *turns, lets go the door, waves, and, to fast harp music, jogs back through the crowd to where it all started!* THE YOUNG MAN, *dismayed, readjusts his face to the situation.*

(*Philosophically*) Well . . . that's how it goes.

He ambles back to the telephone, picks it up, listens.

So I do not yell, threaten, or rouse my blood.

He holds the phone out toward the audience so it can hear the tumult and the shouting inside the earpiece.

Who would hear me?

He hangs up. Silence. The pub lights go out. The pub vanishes.

While I'm waiting at the old house way out in the Irish wild, I take a little drink (*Drinks*), get into my coat and cap (*Does so*), and go out (*Goes*) into the night to look at the clear stars. Until at last, down through the night forest the nineteen-thirty-one Chevrolet comes thrashing, peat-turf-colored on top like Mike himself, and inside the old car—

Through the darkness from stage left comes MIKE, *gliding on a car seat with an apparatus to hold the steering wheel. The car, no more than seat, steering wheel, doors, circles the stage. From it comes the gasping, choking sound of a very old vehicle indeed.* MIKE *and his framework auto stop dead-center stage. The engine, with a hiccup, strangles and dies.*

Mike?

MIKE (*waving easily*)

None other!

THE YOUNG MAN *opens the car door.*

Ain't it a fine warm evenin'?

THE YOUNG MAN (*hesitates; rubs jaw*)
Mike . . . ? Have you ever visited Sicily or Spain? The south of France?

MIKE

No, sir.

THE YOUNG MAN
Paris, the north of France, even?

MIKE

I guess you'd say the furthest south I've ever been is the Tipperary shoreline, sir.

THE YOUNG MAN

I see.

He gets in. He looks at MIKE, *breathes the air, exhales, slams the door.*

Well . . . it's a fine *warm* evening, Mike.

MIKE

You hit it right on the head, sir!

We hear the motor roar, shadows and stars move on the scrim behind them, the men's bodies bounce a little.

THE YOUNG MAN

Mike, how've you been since?

MIKE (*wheeling the car slow and easy*)

Ah, I got me health. Ain't that all-and-everything, with Lent comin' on tomorra?

THE YOUNG MAN (*muses*)

Lent. What will you give up for Lent, Mike?

MIKE

I been turnin' it over. (*Sucks the cigarette which hangs from his lip until his face glows cherry-red*) And why not these terrible things ya see in me mouth?

THE YOUNG MAN

Cigarettes?

MIKE

Dear as gold fillings and a dread congester of the lungs they be! Put it all down, add 'em up, and ya got a sick loss by the year's turnin', ya know. So ya'll not find these filthy creatures in me face again the whole time of Lent—and, who knows, after!

THE YOUNG MAN

Bravo!

MIKE (*suspicious at this outburst; glancing over*)
I see you don't smoke yourself.

THE YOUNG MAN
Forgive me.

MIKE
For what! Bravo, says I to meself if I can wrestle the Devil's
habit two falls out of three!

THE YOUNG MAN
Good luck, Mike.

MIKE
And do you know something? I'll need it!

*We hear the motor roar. The stars over Ireland swirl this way
and that behind the car moving in darkness. At this point,* THE
YOUNG MAN *quietly rises up and steps down from the car and
addresses the audience.*

THE YOUNG MAN
Well, now! We're on our way! But I want to make a few
points . . .

*He reaches out and with one hand swings the car about so it
points its hood and bumpers stage left. The car purrs happily on,*
MIKE *at the wheel, smoking and humming to himself.*

Look upon Mike. The most careful driver in all God's world,
including any sane, small, quiet, butter-and-milk producing
country you'd want to name. Mike, all innocence—a saint!—
when compared to those drivers who switch on paranoia each
time they fuse themselves to their bucket seats in Los Angeles,
Mexico City, or Paris!

*We hear various cars roar by, see flashes of light, hear honking
of horns.* MIKE *philosophically watches the imaginary cars pass,
waving them on with calm good nature.*

Compare him to those blind men who, forsaking tin cups and
white canes, but still wearing their Hollywood dark glasses,

laugh insanely down the Via Veneto in Rome, shaking brake-drum linings like carnival serpentine out their race-car doors!

During the above we hear the approach of a carnival of cars, sput-sputs, hornets, wasps, swarms of big and little blasters and blowers, and mixed with it hilarious voices, shouting, many horns: picnic day at Indianapolis Speedway.

MIKE *smiles at it all, blinking gently, driving along between the bogs. The voices, horns, motors avalanche away into silence.*

THE YOUNG MAN *circles the car, turning it till* MIKE *faces another way, before he continues the lecture.*

But Mike, now . . . See his easy hands loving the wheel in a slow clocklike turning . . .

The car makes a vast, lovely swirl around a bend in the road—we can guess as much by the magical rotation of MIKE's *arms.*

Listen to his mist-breathing voice all night-quiet as he charms the road . . .

MIKE (*singing*)
"As I was walking
Through Dublin City . . .
Around the hour of twelve at night . . ."

THE YOUNG MAN
. . . his foot a tenderly benevolent pat on the whispering accelerator . . .

MIKE (*singing softly*)
"I saw a maid,
So fair was she . . ."

THE YOUNG MAN
. . . never a mile under thirty, never two miles over . . .

MIKE (*singing*)
". . . combing her hair by candlelight."

THE YOUNG MAN *steps back into the car and settles himself, looking kindly on this older man.*

THE YOUNG MAN

Mike, Mike, and his steady boat gentling a mild sweet lake where all Time slumbers. Look: compare. And bind such a man to you with summer grasses, gift him with silver, shake his hand warmly at each journey's end.

MIKE (*reaching for the hand brake*)

Here we are! The Royal Hibernian Hotel!

THE YOUNG MAN

What a fine lilting name!

MIKE (*thinks on it*)

The Royal Hibernian Hotel! Sure, it falls right off the tongue!

THE YOUNG MAN *climbs out.*

THE YOUNG MAN

It does. See you tomorrow, Mike!

The car drives off into darkness.

MIKE

God willing!!

The car is gone. THE YOUNG MAN *turns and walks in a grand circle, vanishing for a moment behind a curtain but reappearing on the instant, checking his watch.*

THE YOUNG MAN

Now. Let twenty-three hours of sleep, breakfast, lunch, supper, late nightcap pass, and here I come again, another midnight . . .

He suits word to action, going in and coming out the door far stage right.

Out the door of that Georgian mansion, to tread down the steps to feel Braillewise in fog for the car which I know bulks there.

*The stage has darkened during part of this speech, and in the
dark, unseen by the audience, the car has returned,* MIKE *in it,
to center stage. We hear the car faintly now. The lights are beginning to come up as* THE YOUNG MAN *gropes forward.*

MIKE

Ah, there you are, sir!

THE YOUNG MAN

Mike. (*To the audience*) I climb in. I give the door its slam.

He slams the door.

And *then* . . .

The car gives a great spasming jerk. THE YOUNG MAN *grabs his
hat, grabs the dashboard, grabs* MIKE'S *knee.*

Mike!

*With a thunderous roar, the car is off, vibrating. The sound is
furious. The black background behind the car rushes and flurries
with lights and shadows; the car spins and turns.*

Mike!

MIKE (smiles benevolently)

Yes, sir.

THE YOUNG MAN

Mike!

MIKE

Yes, *sir!*

THE YOUNG MAN (staring)

Sixty miles an hour, Mike.

MIKE

Seventy!

THE YOUNG MAN

Now it's seventy-five!

MIKE

Is it!

THE YOUNG MAN

Eighty!

MIKE (*looks*)

So it is!

THE YOUNG MAN

Eighty-five! Eighty-five!

MIKE

Can that be possible?

THE YOUNG MAN

It is, it is.

The car turns in a great thunder of shadowy light, in huge riverings of hill and meadow thrown on the backdrop.

THE YOUNG MAN *leaps out and watches the car with* MIKE *bent over the wheel gripping it hard, his smile a leer.*

It is, it was, indeed! There went Mike and me with him! Ninety full miles an hour! From the blazing mouth of the cannon we bounced, skidded, cast ourselves in full stoning ricochet down the paths, over the bogs, through the trees! I felt all Ireland's grass put down its ears when we, with a yell, jumped over a rise!

MIKE

Ninety-five! Do you see that! Ninety-five!

The car whirls, rushes.

THE YOUNG MAN

Mike, I thought—Mike!

MIKE *puffs his cigarette feverishly. Pink light comes and goes on his creased face.*

Mike was changed as if the Adversary himself had squeezed and molded and fired him with a dark hand. There he was, whirling the wheel roundabout, over-around, here we frenzied under trestles, there knocked crossroad signs spinning like weathercocks! I studied Mike's fine face. A fine face no longer!

He moves close. The motor sounds die away so we can hear better, study better. The car still rocks and turns slightly this way and that while THE YOUNG MAN *philosophizes, standing beside it, perhaps pointing in at* MIKE's *face with a flashlight.*

The wisdom drained from it. The eyes, neither gentle nor philosophical. The mouth neither tolerant nor at peace. It was a face washed raw, a scalded peeled potato.

Thunder up for a moment. Flashing lights. MIKE *leans avidly forward. The thunder fades.* THE YOUNG MAN *is back in the car now.*

MIKE (*loud, raucous*)
Well, how you been since, sir!

THE YOUNG MAN
Mike, your voice! It's changed!

MIKE
Changed?!

THE YOUNG MAN (*to the audience*)
A clarion, a trumpet, all iron and brassy tin! Gone the warm fire. Gone the gentle grass. (*To* MIKE *now*) Mike, has a dire thing come into your life, a sickness, a sorrow, a sore affliction?

MIKE (*amazed, loud*)
Now why would you think that?

THE YOUNG MAN (*touches the car*)
And, Mike, is this the same car you drove last night?

MIKE
None other!

THE YOUNG MAN (*to the audience*)
But it was changed, too. This car, this crusty old beggar that had been content to stroll along, careful of its breath and bones, now thundered toward Hell as if to warm itself at some special blaze there.

THE YOUNG MAN *scans* MIKE *now, carefully.*

Hold on, I got it! Mike! It's the first night of Lent!

MIKE

It is, sir.

THE YOUNG MAN

Well, then, remembering your Lenten promise, why's that cigarette in your mouth?

MIKE *casts his eyes down on the smoke jiggling on his lip and shrugs.*

MIKE

Ah—I give up the *ither.*

There is a long moment during which THE YOUNG MAN *stares.*

THE YOUNG MAN

The other?

MIKE (*nodding wisely*)

The ither.

THE YOUNG MAN *pulls as far back in his seat as possible to look at* MIKE. *Suddenly he reaches forward and twists the key in the ignition. With a great squealing,* MIKE *brings the car to a halt, surprised but not angry.*

Why, will you tell me, did you do that?

In silence, the two sit there.

THE YOUNG MAN

Mike, for two hundred nights we have ridden together.

MIKE

True.

THE YOUNG MAN

And each night as I came from my employer's house I drank, at the door, a fiery douse of Scotch or bourbon "against the chill."

MIKE

A reasonable precaution.

THE YOUNG MAN

Then I walked out to this cab where sat a man, yourself, who,
during all the long winter evening's wait for me to phone for
your services, had *lived* in Heeber Finn's pub.

MIKE

You might say, it's me office!

THE YOUNG MAN (*slaps his own brow*)

Fool!

MIKE

Who is?

THE YOUNG MAN

I am!

MIKE

And why?

THE YOUNG MAN

Because, Mike, because there in Heeber Finn's while you waited,
you took onto yourself—a mellowness. And that mellowness dis-
tilled itself down in a slow rain that damped your smoldering
nerves. It colored your cheeks, warmed your eyes soft, lowered
your voice to a husking mist, and spread in your chest to slow
your heart to a gentle jog-trot.

MIKE

Ah, I wish the Guinness family could hear you!

THE YOUNG MAN

It loosened your hands on the wheel and sat you with grace and
ease as you gentled us through fogs and mists that kept us and
Dublin apart. And all the while, Mike, the liquor *I* drank
stopped me from ever detecting the scent of any spirits on *your*
breath.

MIKE

What are you leading up to, sir?

THE YOUNG MAN

This, Mike! Tonight, the first night of Lent, for the first time in all the nights I've driven with you, you are sober!

He lets this sink in. MIKE *lets it sink in, too, aghast.*

MIKE

By God now, that's true.

THE YOUNG MAN

And all those other two hundred nights you weren't driving slow and careful and easy just for my safety—

MIKE

Well——

THE YOUNG MAN

—but because of the gentle warm spirits sloping now on this side, now on that side of you, as we took the long scything curves.

MIKE (*as if revealing something*)

If you *must* know, yes; I *was* drunk all of them nights.

They both sit and look at each other for a long moment.

THE YOUNG MAN

And now you've given up liquor for Lent?

MIKE (*nods righteously*)

You've noticed the improvement?

There is a moment of critical silence.

THE YOUNG MAN

Drive on, Mike.

MIKE *starts the car with a roar. They thunder on, rocking silently,* THE YOUNG MAN *studying the older.*

MIKE

And here we are! Dublin's Fair City!

He stops the car. THE YOUNG MAN *gets thoughtfully out. He looks around at the imaginary city. He speaks to the audience.*

THE YOUNG MAN

Dublin's fair city. Oh, who *really* knows the Irish, say I, and which half of them is which? Mike? (*Turns to look at the man*) Which Mike is the real Mike? Which is the Mike that *everyone* knows? (*Gasps, shakes his head as at a foul vision*) I will not think on it. There is only one Mike for me. That one that Ireland shaped herself with her weathers and waters, her seedings and harvestings, her brans and mashes, her brews, bottlings, and swiggings. If you ask what makes the Irish what they are, I'd point on down the road (*Points*) and tell where you turn to find Heeber Finn's. (*Turns*) Mike?

MIKE

Sir?

THE YOUNG MAN

Wait here a second!

THE YOUNG MAN *runs offstage. He comes running back out a moment later, something hidden under his coat.*

Will you do me a favor, Mike?

MIKE

Name it!

THE YOUNG MAN *winces at the loudness of that voice.*

THE YOUNG MAN

Here.

MIKE

What's that, sir?

MIKE *blinks at the bottle* THE YOUNG MAN *has brought from hiding.*

THE YOUNG MAN

A bottle of whisky.

MIKE

I rarely see a whole bottle of it. That's why I didn't recognize—

THE YOUNG MAN

Mike, this is the first night of Lent, right? Now . . . on the second night of Lent—

MIKE

Tomorrow night?

THE YOUNG MAN

On the second night of Lent, when you come to pick me up, in Kilcock, will you *drink* this, Mike?

MIKE

Do you know what you're doing?

THE YOUNG MAN

Tempting you, Mike.

MIKE (*sore torn between*)

You are indeed.

THE YOUNG MAN

Take it, Mike.

MIKE

Ah, God, it's Lent.

THE YOUNG MAN

Only the first night.

MIKE

You said that before, but with repetition it makes sense.

THE YOUNG MAN

Give something *else* up!

MIKE

Ah, Jesus, in all of Ireland, there's not so much joy, beauty, and riotous pleasure about you can count them on more than five fingers! Gimme the damn thing!

THE YOUNG MAN

Good old Mike!

MIKE (*eyeing the bottle*)

Do I drink it *all?*

THE YOUNG MAN

Or as much as will turn Mr. Hyde into Dr. Jekyll!

MIKE

How's that?

THE YOUNG MAN (*rephrasing it*)

Enough so Mike will come for me tomorrow night, instead of you.

MIKE

Mike instead of *me? I'm* Mike. Michael Finneran Seamus Kelly!

THE YOUNG MAN

Are you?

He peers in at the fellow. MIKE *gets his meaning, uncorks the bottle, takes a long swig.*

MIKE

Ah!

He takes another swig as THE YOUNG MAN *beams.* MIKE *leans out, his voice immediately softer, mellower.*

Is that better?

THE YOUNG MAN

Mike, Mike you're back!

MIKE (*nods slowly*)

I was long away.

THE YOUNG MAN

You were!

They clench hands in a great shake, steadfast, true.

MIKE

Here now, take these precious bits of pure gold!

He shoves over his cigarette pack.

THE YOUNG MAN (*taking them*)

Thanks, Mike.

MIKE (*gently*)

Ah, shut up.

THE YOUNG MAN

See you tomorrow?

MIKE

If we're both alive.

THE YOUNG MAN

Do you doubt we will be?

MIKE (*with a last swig*)

Strange—I'm thinking now—I'll live forever.

He drives off, waving beautifully. THE YOUNG MAN *watches the car go. He lights one of* MIKE's *cigarettes, studies it, studies the smoke on the air.*

THE YOUNG MAN

The Irish? The Irish. Here they come out of the mist. There they vanish into the rain.

He calls into the growing darkness.

Michael Finneran Seamus Kelly! *Who* and *what* are *you*?

He listens.

No answer. And (*Checks watch*)—already, look! It's the *second* day of Lent! So—what am *I* giving up?

He looks at the cigarette pack, rips it open.

What indeed?!

He tears the cigarettes apart, sprinkles the tobacco about, beaming. A harp plays in the darkness offstage. THE YOUNG MAN, *hearing it, laughs and shrugs.*

All right, all right! Let the harp play all it wants! I'm done, finished, through!

He moves briskly for the exit stage right as the harp lilts up playing a zestful reel. Just before exiting, THE YOUNG MAN *turns about once, and maybe clicks his heels. When he is gone, from the darkness* MIKE *reappears on his throne, in his car, swinging back out in one long wonderful slow curve.* MIKE's *smile is mellow. The motor is quiet. The harp plays gently now, as* MIKE *vanishes back into the Irish dark, and on away toward . . .*

THE END

A Clear View of an Irish Mist

CHARACTERS

HEEBER FINN
KATHLEEN (HIS WIFE)
OLD MAN
CASEY
TIMULTY
NOLAN
FATHER LEARY
HOOLIHAN (THE SALESMAN)
NOONAN
O'HARA
KELLY

At the rise of curtain we see the bar of Heeber Finn's pub some-where deep in Ireland's fogs and rains, deserted in the early-morning hour. For a change, a rosy glare comes through the stained-glass windows to either side of the bar; the day has be-gun with rare weather.

HEEBER FINN *enters, breathing the good air, scratching him-self, yawning, fully dressed for a day of business. He looks about at the silent room.*

FINN

Ah, there you are, waiting for it all to begin. What will happen today? Only God knows in the morning. By ten tonight *I'll* know. Some day I should set it down.

He moves about, arranging the chairs.

HIS WIFE (*entering*)

Set what down?

FINN

All that happens, Katy, in a single day with the doors open and the world flocking in.

HIS WIFE

Would you rather write it or live it?

FINN

Since you put it that way—living's best.

HIS WIFE

Live and *work.* I wish you'd do more of that. There's much needs mending here. That chair leans favoring the left, the table leans favoring the right. . . .

FINN (*polishing*)

Playing with these spigots is my work!

69

HIS WIFE

And you play them fine, like the organist at the Variety Cinema in Cork, but—

FINN

But, Woman! It's opening time!

HIS WIFE (*checking*)

Ten seconds after.

FINN (*hustling*)

Wait till I get set up! Peep through the door! What do you see?

She peeps.

HIS WIFE

A band of hoodlums, as is usual, elbowing each other and smacking their lips.

FINN

Well, what are you waiting for?

HIS WIFE (*peeking through a chink*)

It does me good to make them stay out in the cold a bit overtime.

FINN

You've a hard heart!

HIS WIFE

I thought you only worried about my soft behind.

She fiddles with the latch. There is a groan of relief from outside.

Ah, listen to them craitures stir, will ya? Like so many cows in need of milking!

She fiddles the latch again, smiling. Another groan from outside.

They're fairly seething!

FINN

Inhuman woman, let be!

She unlocks, unbolts, and lets the Red Sea in.

HIS WIFE

One at a time! No hurry!

THE OLD MAN (*entering indignant*)

One at a time? No hurry? What does she mean?

CASEY

Out of the way, Woman!

TIMULTY

Lift me to the bar, I'm too weak to make it alone!

NOLAN

I'm famished!

FINN

Come get it, Men!

THE OLD MAN

Finn, why the delay? You opened twenty seconds late!

HIS WIFE (*snorting*)

Twenty seconds! The shame of it!

She exits.

THE OLD MAN

Has she got the humors?

FINN

When *hasn't* she?

NOLAN

Women!

THE OLD MAN

I'm glad you said that. Why is it, when a ship goes down, it's always women and children first to the lifeboats? Shouldn't it be the other way round?

CASEY

Oh, my wife wouldn't mind going down with the ship. The question is: Would the ship mind going down with *her?*

THE OLD MAN

I think we have found a proper subject to converse on for the day.

All drink, assenting.

CASEY

Break out the cards, we'll have a game!

All move away into the next room, dragging chairs, flourishing a deck of cards, carrying their drinks, laughing and warmly joyous. After the brief riot, there is a little storm of silence in the pub. THE WIFE *appears with a basket, on her way out to shop. She peers into the next room, sniffs.*

HIS WIFE

Well, the avalanche is fair started down the mountain!

FINN *eyes her but she will not be eyed and goes off, away.*
    Another silent moment. FINN *polishes glassware. Then:*
    The doors open. It is FATHER LEARY, *from the church across the way.*

FINN

Father Leary, come in! We don't see you often!

FATHER

I'm glad to hear that. I was beginning to worry.

FINN

Will it be the Same?

FATHER

First you say you don't see me often, then you ask if it'll be the Same!

FINN

No offense, Father. What'll it be?

FATHER

The Usual.

FINN (*pouring*)

Begging your pardon, Father, but what's the difference between the *Same* and the *Usual?*

FATHER (*drinking*)

Same is too blunt, cold, hard a word. *Usual* is—well—more savory, at ease, you can roll it about on your tongue. (*He savors the word*) Us–u–al. Do you see?

FINN

As far as I need to, Father. And how's business? I mean—the Church, are people finding their way there through all the fog lately?

FATHER

If they don't, I'll build hellfires to give them light.

FINN

Oh, you can do that, all right. You know, Father, I was thinking just the other day, you and me—is much alike. No offense.

FATHER (*pausing in midsip*)

It's too early to tell. Go on.

FINN

I mean, the things you hear in the confessional and the things I hear behind the bar. There is a rough equivalation, now.

FATHER

Very rough.

FINN (sotto voce)

And neither of us can *breathe a word.*

FATHER

Come now, Finn, you'll be putting on lace next.

FINN

Father, no word that's spoken goes back across this bar. I'm proud of my own peculiar vow of silence. If the church ain't open, Heeber Finn's is.

FATHER (*controlling himself beautifully*)

You must be absolutely groaning with truckloads of sin.

FINN

I got me share.

FATHER

You don't imply now, do you, that you're in competition with the Church? Eh?

FINN

Heaven forbid! And forgive my pride, but maybe I've eased your burden a bit, Father.

FATHER

Do you mean by that that some sins get waylaid here that I never hear about?

FINN

I only imply, Father, that I oil their tonsils so they can tell it better by the time they get over to you, thus cutting down the fearsome time you spend cooped up in the box—

FATHER

Why, you're almost an annex to the Church, it seems!

FINN

Now look what I've done—made you mad.

FATHER

I'm not mad, Finn, just surprised, and mad at myself . . . for I thought I was over being surprised at the duplicity of man. You did come on me sudden, though, and I'd best leave.

He reaches in his pocket.

FINN (*hastily*)

Put it in the poorbox, Father.

FATHER

I will!

FINN

Come again for the—er—Usual, Father!

Half out the door, FATHER LEARY *turns, frowning.*

FATHER

Not the *Usual,* man! (*A beat*)—The *Same!*

The wickets slam. He's gone.

FINN *busies himself, stacking glasses and wiping the bar. As he does so, from a distance a high clear tenor voice is heard, approaching. There is also the sound of footsteps coming near. The song being sung is as follows:*

THE SALESMAN'S VOICE (*Off*)

"All through life
Mid storm and strife . . .
With maid or wife,
It's the thinkin'
Not the drinkin'
Makes it go."

The voice stops. The wickets open. A SALESMAN *stands looking in and about the pub.*

FINN *has frozen at the words of the song. He does not turn now as the stranger advances easily toward the bar.*

THE SALESMAN

Though I must admit, there be occasions when the very wheels of Juggernaut are kept turning with drink. A Guinness, please.

This friendly sally does not unfreeze FINN *at all; he draws the drink without looking up.*

THE SALESMAN *looks at* FINN *and senses diplomacy is needed.*

I see that your spine is all one piece because of my song.

FINN (*turning at last*)
The song was a touch subversive of my business.

THE SALESMAN (*sings*)
"It's the thinkin'
And the drinkin'
Makes it go."
   Is that better?

FINN (*putting the drink on the bar*)
Why didn't you sing it that way to start?

THE SALESMAN
I'm a proud man.

FINN (*letting the drink go*)
Pride's no sin, if it has to do with your business. What line are you in?

THE SALESMAN
I guess you'd call me a Salesman of Philosophy.

FINN
Now, how do you sell *that*?

THE SALESMAN
Here!
He swings a small case onto the bar.

Do you know the saying "Infinite riches in a little room"?

FINN
I know it now.

THE SALESMAN
Well, in this little case is the "furniture" I'm selling.

FINN
For a doll house, then?

THE SALESMAN

No, to decorate the palace of man's mind!

He opens up the case and puts forth a single item on the counter.

FINN (*confounded*)

That's *it?*

THE SALESMAN (*proudly*)

That's it! Fine hand-painted bone porcelain.

FINN

Don't look like much to me. (*Moving around front*) Furniture, you say.

He stops. He approaches the little object slowly, peering at it. It is about eight inches long and three inches high. There is a single word on it, a word in white letters on a black background.

(*Spelling out loud*) T . . . H . . . it says . . . I and N and K. THINK! Is that all?

THE SALESMAN

I'm inclined to say it's everything!

FINN (*half-suspicious*)

What does it *mean?*

THE SALESMAN

Just what it says, friend. Think. *Think.* THINK!

THE SALESMAN's *voice grows in timbre and volume each time he says the word. Then he subsides and sips his Guinness.*

FINN (*uneasily*)

Ye-ess, I see what you're getting at. But what do you do with a bit of furniture like that? To what purpose is it?

THE SALESMAN

To what purpose? God save me!

Before FINN *can stop him, he is around the bar and placing the little sign on top of a Guinness barrel.*

There! Now, pretend you're your own best customer, and I'm yourself, the bartender. You got your drink in your hand.

He nudges the drink. FINN *takes and holds the glass.*

You sip your drink.

FINN *sips.*

You raise your eyes——

FINN *raises his eyes.*

And what do you see?

> FINN

"Think"?

> THE SALESMAN

Right! You drink some more.

FINN *drinks.*

You stare at that little sign . . . and . . . first thing you know . . . you're . . .

> FINN

Thinking!

> THE SALESMAN

Ah, now you got the sun up. You're standing in the light!

> FINN (*sips, stares; sips, stares*)

Ah . . . ah . . . yes . . . I see.

> THE SALESMAN

I *know* you *do!*

FINN *looks at the man with fresh admiration.*

> FINN

You be a kind of intellectual, then?

> THE SALESMAN

I—er—*knocked* at the door of Trinity College!

> FINN

What stopped your plunging through?

THE SALESMAN *refills both glasses, playing bartender with a fine air.*

THE SALESMAN

Well, I shaped it up in my mind. Hoolihan, I said to myself, why put off helping others half your life? Why not start this day? How? I said. Well, I said, what's mainly wrong with the world? What? I said. No one stops to think any more, I said. And for lack of stopping to think, what happens?

FINN (*leaning toward him*)

A great lot, one supposes.

THE SALESMAN

Wars, famines, depressions, murderous impulses, bad livers, short breaths, unwanted children, and marriages best kept running on whisky for fear of seeing the true aspect!

FINN (*enchanted*)

Say that again.

THE SALESMAN

If you don't mind, I'll let the echoes die.

FINN

Right! That's a beautiful thing there, the little bit of porcelain and that single word. Already I feel a popping in my ears, like I'm on a mountain! It's amazing how full of thoughts I suddenly am.

THE SALESMAN

Think what it'll do for your customers, then, and the brand of talk they'll spray at one another! In one hour, in this room, the humidity will rise ten points!

FINN

All I do is leave it set right there, eh?

THE SALESMAN

Right there. Nothing to wind, nothing to grease or oil, nothing to get out of whack. A simple machine it is, and'll make men's minds *"GO"!*

FINN

I'll take one! Wait! You *are* selling them, aren't you?

THE SALESMAN

Not exactly. You can rent this for just ten shillings a month!

FINN

That's dear!

THE SALESMAN

If it raises your business twenty shillings a month, you're still ten ahead!

FINN (*amazed*)

Will it *do* that?

THE SALESMAN

Who can deny thinking men blow off steam, and what makes steam? Water! And what is beer and ale and stout but mostly water?

FINN

You've gone below the surface, I see.

THE SALESMAN

Study pays. Try it. If it don't work out after four weeks, I'll buy the damn thing off you at half-price or—er—thereabouts; you'll be little out of pocket!

FINN *is still grudging.*

Hold on, let me sweeten the deal.

He pulls forth three more objects and sets them up on the bar.

Rent one, you get them all!

FINN *stares.*

FINN (*reading*)
STOP! CONSIDER! THINK! DO!

THE SALESMAN

Ain't that a fine quartet?

FINN

Explain them to me!

THE SALESMAN

Well, before you can *THINK,* you got to *CONSIDER* what you want to think about, right?

FINN (*nods*)

The fog parts.

THE SALESMAN

After you consider what to think and think it, thinking's no good, is it, if you don't *DO?*

FINN

By God, you're right. You might as well arrange a flower bouquet and throw it in the River Liffey as think and not *do.* But you've not explained the first—

THE SALESMAN

The first is *most* important! You must *STOP* whatever else you're doing, scratching your ear and notching your belt or whatever, mustn't you, in order to *CONSIDER THINKING* and *DOING?*

FINN

That's it, bull's-eye on! I'll take the lot!

FINN *gestures frantically, for he is still "customer" outside the bar, while behind the bar is* THE SALESMAN.

Ring up *No Sale* and take out ten shillings before I regain my sanity!

THE SALESMAN *is to the register like a shot. Bang! A bell rings, the red* NO SALE *sign jumps up.*

THE SALESMAN

How about another?

                              FINN
Don't mind if I do!

THE SALESMAN *pours for both. They hoist them.*

                         THE SALESMAN
To the Brave New World of this afternoon!

                              FINN
So soon?

                         THE SALESMAN
You'll note the difference within hours. To thought-provocation,
to the pub called *Heeber Finn's,* to the Oracle at Delphi in a
way, to this cavern of philosophers—

                              FINN
Tavern of philosophers—that has a ring to it.

                         THE SALESMAN
Cavern.

                         FINN (*nettled*)
Cavern's what I said! A cavern brimming over with philosophers,
eh?

                    THE WIFE (*walking through*)
Philosophers? Is that the same as hoboes?

She is gone.

                         THE SALESMAN
Who was that?

                         FINN (*eyes shut*)
I dread to tell you.

               THE SALESMAN (*nods understandingly*)
(*Recovers briskly*) To Finn's then, where people stop! consider!
think! and *do!*

FINN

I'll drink to *those* damn things, any day.

They drink.

THE SALESMAN (*walking*)

Well, I'll be off!

FINN (*worried*)

You won't sell any more of these in the village, now?

THE SALESMAN

Nor in the next. I like to drop one stone in the pond and watch the lovely ripples—*spread!* (*He illustrates*)

FINN (*awed*)

Your father was a poet.

THE SALESMAN (*eyebrows up*)

Uncanny! You guessed it! Good day!

FINN

And a fine one to *you*, Hoolihan!

HOOLIHAN *exits.*

THE SALESMAN (*singing*)

"In life, in strife,
With maid, or wife
It's the *thinking,*
Not the drinking,
Makes it . . . *Go!*"

He is gone.

  Now FINN, *alone, exhales with pleasure. He mops off each of the little ceramic signs, exhales on them, shines them again—then, like a painter, looks about at the empty bar, looking left, left center, center, right center, right.*

FINN (*to himself*)

Now where is best for each . . . ? Well . . .

He snatches one and places it far over at stage right. The sign reads STOP!

When they come in the door they should see this right off!

What's next? Well, when their little eyes move on over along, the next thing they should see is *CONSIDER,* right? Right!

He places CONSIDER right center.

New let's think where to put *THINK.*

He picks THINK up, deliberates, puts it back down on top the Guinness tap-barrel.

Right where he had it is best! And last of all, *DO* should go over by the door on the other side, so people, on the way out, will *do* things. Right? I think it is!

He locates DO where he has said he'd put it and stands back again to survey his tasks finished.

   At which point his WIFE *happens through. He flinches as if he had expected her to throw scalding water on him and makes elaborately casual attempts to look calm, collected, and not guilty of putting out hard money for strange devices.*

   He saunters toward the bar, turning in a circle past his WIFE, *who also turns in a circle, suspicious of the smell of him.*

THE WIFE

Well?

He reaches the bar, polishes the first sign, STOP!

FINN

Well, indeed!

He moves over to polish the second, CONSIDER. She turns away and huffs out. He flings down the rag.

Damn, she didn't see! Or did she see and disapprove? All right, steady, Finn, a calm mind in a calm body, eh? (*Pours*) Here's calmness. (*Drinks*) Ah.

*At which point the doors fling wide, and a man enters, somewhat
in his cups. He freezes and stares.*

FINN *looks at the man, follows his gaze to see what he is
looking at and finds it is the sign:* STOP!

*The man sways there a moment, blinking, debating, then
wheels about.*

I——

The man charges back out, gone.

Now, what the——? Well, where was I? Oiling the stormy seas.
Another drop of oil, eh?

*He gives himself a drop. He rearranges one of the signs, smiles
at it, pats it.*

*The same half-drunk man enters again, is again transfixed at
what he sees, wheels, and goes out.*

I'll be . . . Now that's most peculiar. That *was* Tom Noonan,
wasn't it? (*Shrugs*) Ah, he'll be back.

We can see NOONAN, *outside, warming up for another try. He
steels himself, takes a deep breath, and bursts through the doors
again. He is half across the barroom floor, at full steam, when
his eyes fix to the dire sign and he cries in loud dismay, almost a
wail:*

NOONAN

Stop!

*and circles around to flail out and is gone again, this time for
good.*

FINN (*going after him*)

Tom Noonan, oh, *Tom!* (*stops, bewildered*) Gone. Did he say
"Stop"? Yes. Must have misunderstood. That one sign wasn't
meant for *him.*

He goes over and peers at the sign.

(*Muses*) Stop . . .

He is wracked with indecision. He picks up the sign, puts it down, picks it up again.

Well, it might be best, for the first few hours, anyway, to turn this one around so no one can see it, right off. Later, I'll turn it back. It's not really the most important sign, anyway, is it? No!

He turns the sign around so we can't read it.

There! Now we still have (*Points*) CONSIDER! THINK! DO! (*Rubs hands*) All right, world, I'm ready for you! I'd best tell the boys to come in and—

FATHER LEARY *enters, or rather, almost backs in through the door.*

There you are, Father Leary!

FATHER (*bemused*)
Am I? So I am. On my way to Mrs. Kelly's I just saw Tom Noonan on the street.

FINN (*suddenly uneasy*)
Noonan? Tom?

FATHER
Run up to me and insisted right there on the curb I take his confession!

FINN (*attempting cheer*)
Did he? That's nice.

FATHER
Nice, but not like Tom. He wouldn't take no. Held onto my elbow, he did. So I shut my eyes and pretended not to know and heard him out!

FINN
Fast thinking, Father!

FATHER
The Archbishop would jump straight up if he heard.

FINN
I won't tell him.

FATHER (*looking sharp*)

Do you *know* him?

FINN (*pulling his horns in*)

Now that you mention it, no . . .

FATHER (*baffled*)

It was over in a trice and Noonan gone. Said he'd stop this and
stop that and stop two of those and three of the next-worst. I
can't tell you *what* he said he'd stop, of course, but stop it was,
all up and down the line.

FINN *has backed over to the counter to hide the sign with his
back. He is edgy.*

FINN

Think of *that*.

FATHER

I *am* thinking of it, Finn.

FINN *has the "machine," the sign, in his hands behind his back
now.*

What's that behind your back, Finn?

FINN

Why, Father, it's—

Crash! The damn thing has fallen to the floor. FINN *turns to look
at the shards. He bends to pick them up.*

Why, it's kind of a—jigsaw puzzle, Father.

FATHER

I like puzzles.

FINN

Ah, you couldn't work this one—

FATHER

Let me try.

FINN *reluctantly puts the pieces on the bar.*

That don't look so difficult, now, Finn.

FINN (*to himself*)

More's the pity.

FATHER

Eh?

FINN

Will you have a drink while you work it, Father?

FATHER (*working*)

This piece would seem to go here . . . Eh? Yes, Finn, bless
you, man . . . and this piece here. . . .

FINN *pours.* FATHER LEARY *tinkers.*

. . . as I was saying. Noonan now . . . right on the street!
Nothing wrong really, I suppose, confessing him in the open,
God's everywhere . . . but still . . . it shook me . . . why
should old *Tom?* Stop *this* I will! he said, and stop *that!* and stop
the others! (*He tinkers with the bits*) Put this piece over here
. . . and move this about . . . There . . . it seems to be a
word, Finn.

FINN (*mock surprise*)

Fancy that.

LEARY *shoves some more bits about.*

FATHER

S would seem to be the first letter of the puzzle.

FINN

Are you sure?

FATHER

S . . . T—that's a T, ain't it? (*He moves a last shard in place*)
O . . . P.

FINN (*brightly*)

"Stop!"

FATHER (*disquieted*)

I can read, Finn.

FINN

I've always spoke well of your education, sir.

FATHER (*musing*)

"Stop," Finn. *Stop.* Have you heard that word before in the last three minutes?

FINN

You may have used it, sir.

FATHER

Tom Noonan, didn't *he* use it, too?

FINN

We mustn't talk of it, Father. The vows of the confessional—

FATHER

Finn!

FINN (*quietly*)

Yes, sir?

FATHER

Was Tom Noonan in here lately?

FINN

Of recent date, Father?

FATHER

Date, hell, man. The last hour?

FINN

Well, in and out, Father.

FATHER

Which is it, in *or* out?

FINN

It became a trifle circuitous, Father, to coin a word.

FATHER

Circuitous? Do you infer he weaved in circles, then?

FINN

I only infer, Father, he made one arc coming and another going. Six arcs in all, Father.

FATHER

Broken down, you say he arrived three times—

FINN

And left just as many—

FATHER

In how long a time?

FINN

It was remarkable for its shortness, Father. He came and went, arrived and departed, came through the entrance and looked for the exit.

FATHER (*toying with the reconstructed sign*)

How do you account for his behavior, Finn?

FINN

His wife had been nagging him, sir.

FATHER

And?

FINN

And he had been drinking hard at it, down the road, I suppose, at Rooney's pub.

FATHER

Go on.

FINN

And they heaved him out, no doubt, and he came up this way seeking more of the Same or the Usual, begging your pardon, Father. And when he came in the door, I can only figure he saw this sign, sir.

FATHER

This *sign* made him go out and in three times, and then run to me to confess in broad daylight?

FINN

Yes, sir. I figure for thirty years now, Noonan's wife has yelled at him, STOP this, STOP that! STOP the next best and the least-worst and the half-between. "STOP!" she yells. But mostly *STOP DRINKING!* It adds up, down the years. Well, today, Noonan hears "STOP!" from Rooney's bar, too, STOP! no more ale, whisky, or whatever, STOP! and threw him out! So he comes up here, shell-shocked, it's reached the point, after thirty years of his wife screaming and Rooney yelling. And he comes in the door and what does he see?

FATHER

S–T–O–P.

FINN

Right, Father. And that made a little drive-shaft go loose in Noonan and he headed straight off for you, sir.

FATHER

You sound rather proud of the whole thing, Finn.

FINN

Shouldn't I be, Father? A thirty-year sinner reformed? A lost soul changed—?

FATHER (*impatiently*)

Ah, let be! (*muses*) Finn?

FINN

Sir?

FATHER

I don't know how to explain it, but I have this unearthly sensa-tion, lately, each time I drop by that some day I'll come in and find you selling Bibles and holding services.

FINN

Perish the thought, Father. I just redecorated the place a bit.

He waves his hand at the other signs.

FATHER (*staring*)

God help us, don't tell me there's more? (*Squints*) Does that
say *CONSIDER*, Finn?

FINN

It does.

FATHER

And that *THINK*, and that one *DO*?

FINN

What eyes, for a man your age!

FATHER

Is fifty *old*, Finn?

FINN

It's neither in nor out of the casket. You'll be around a while,
Father.

FATHER

I will, Finn, I will. And now suppose you tell me what these signs
mean?

FINN (*trying to recall the spiel*)

Well, *CONSIDER* means . . . walk around, turn about . . .
run your hand, run your eyes over a thing . . .

FATHER

What thing, Finn?

FINN

Anything, sir.

FATHER

Did it ever strike you, Finn, that maybe there are some things
should not be considered at all?

FINN

Like what, sir?

FATHER

Well, fornication, for one, if you force me to it!

FINN

That's a brave start, sir.

FATHER

Poverty's another. It must be borne, not considered. If you have
no coal and no way to get coal and *never will have any coal,* as
often happens at the church, believe me, I do not *consider* coal!
Women, Mr. Finn, can have no part in my life, so I do not
consider women. Travel, I will never travel, so I do not *consider*
palm trees and sandy beaches and twanging guitars. And since
I do not consider the above subjects as fit, to begin with, that
takes us on to your next sign, Finn: *THINK.* Since I will not
consider certain subjects to start with, that means they never
become objects of my thought. I do not *THINK* about them.

FINN

That's what the salesman said, you got to consider first, pick a
subject, before you can *THINK* about it.

FATHER

He was right. And thus, through disconsideration and unthought-
fulness, Finn, I am never tempted to climb the ladder of a stocking—

FINN

Father, you shock me!

FATHER

Sorry! Ladder of a *silk* stocking! Nor do I perspire for straw-
berry shortcakes, breathe hard for swimming in warm equatorial
waters, or ask for more than this rough stuff on my back. If you
consider too much, you think too much, and if you think too
much you wind up *DOING,* Finn. Doing. Doing!

FINN

You're right, Father, that's how women, and other things, get
done.

FATHER

Finn!

FINN

Sorry. It was off my tongue before I knew.

FATHER

It was! Now! (*The gimlet eye*) The salesman that sold you these, was he from the *north* of Ireland?

FINN

I think not.

FATHER

Were these articles *made* in Orange territory?

FINN

Why don't we look, sir?

He hastens the three objects over and puts them down before FATHER LEARY, *who peers.*

What do you see, Father?

FATHER

Hold on, I left my glasses at the rectory.

FINN

Borrow mine, Father—here!

He holds them out. FATHER LEARY *hesitates.*

Don't be afraid, Father. You won't see the world much different through these than through your own.

FATHER

I wouldn't be so sure, Finn! Do you see near or far?

FINN

A bit of both, Father. But it's best I leave the damn things off. Without my glasses, the world looks fine, sinners look less like Africans and more like angels, the shadows they cast are short and sweet, and the sun stays up till midnight.

FATHER

God help us, that kind of vision would turn a trough full of pigs into the Last Supper. Put your glasses on, man, and keep them on!

FINN

It's best to be a little blind in this sharp world, Father.

FATHER

Shut up, and give me the loan.

LEARY *gets the spectacles at last, puts them on, peers at the "machines."*

FINN

Well, *were* they made in the north of Ireland?

FATHER

No, the western part of the U.S.A.

FINN

That's good, Father.

FATHER

Is *California* good, Finn?

FINN

The north or the south of California, sir?

FATHER (*squints*)

A town with the name of—Alhambra!

FINN (*truly enlightened*)

Alhambra! Ain't that Spanish? And aren't the Spanish Catholic?

FATHER

They're a *variety* of Catholic, you might say.

FINN

Might? I always thought Catholic was Catholic!

FATHER

Finn, you talk like a blatherin' infant! There's types and sizes.
There's Eye-talian Catholic, which is pretty good.

FINN

It is indeed!

FATHER

There's Spanish Catholic, which is fair.

FINN

Only fair?

FATHER

And there's French Catholics, which is hardly Catholic at all.
It is rock-bottom Catholic, the fringe elements of the Church.
Now if you want your *real* Catholic, it's here in Ireland he lives.
Not that we don't sin; we do. Not that we're perfect; we're not.
But there be varieties and varieties of Catholic, never forget, and
the sad reflection of my life is there was never a Pope named
Patrick!

FINN (*philosophically*)

Ah, well, we had a Saint!

FATHER

I'm grateful, don't misunderstand.

FINN (*peering*)

Alhambra, California, sounds Catholic enough to me.

FATHER

Do you have the facts and figures on church attendance in Alhambra, California, close at hand, Finn?

FINN

I do not, Father.

FATHER

Then button your lip and fill my glass.

FINN

What'll it be, Father, the Same or the Usual?

FATHER LEARY *glares.* FINN *subsides.* FATHER LEARY *peers.*

FATHER

It says The Monongaheela Gimcrack Novelty Company Inc. Monongaheela? That's pagan Indian, ain't it?

FINN

I wouldn't be surprised, Father.

FATHER

Are you *ever* surprised, Finn?

FINN

Like you, very rarely any more, Father.

FATHER

I wish you'd stop teaming us up, Finn. (*Reads*) "A Little of Something for Everybody" is the motto of this manufactory in Alhambra, California.

FINN (*savoring it*)

"A Little of Something for Everybody"——

FATHER

Now, if that doesn't sound like the title for a Protestant sermon, I never heard one—

FINN

Oh, now, Father—

FATHER

Mind you, I don't say this manufactory put these signs out to make trouble in the world. No, far from it. In all innocence, I think they thought they was putting out lovely little mottoes such as *GOD BLESS OUR HOME,* which they were not. I forgive them their blind fumbling, Finn. But think of the misery they have probably spread in the world wherever these signs be!

FINN

I'm thinking on it. And I'm filled with remorse. You see, that salesman, he talked as good as you, Father. Yes, he did, he had a fine tongue, and first thing I knew I had the fevers.

FATHER

You know what you have to do now, Finn?

FINN

What, sir?

FATHER LEARY *nods at the three items on the bar, holds out his hand.*

(*Groans*) Oh, no.

FATHER

Oh, yes, Finn.

FINN

But I've only had them an hour, it's not been a true test, sir!

FATHER

Which is more important, the philosophy of this small town deep in green Ireland, or tuppence-hapenny?

FINN

I wish it *was* tuppence-hapenny, sir. Father, look—

He hands over the shards and one sign.

Take *STOP* and *CONSIDER* with you. Leave *THINK* and *DO* with me.

FATHER

Finn—

FINN

At the first sign of outbreak, unease, riot, or so much as a headache on the part of a villager, Father, you'll see these flying through the air onto the stones!

FATHER

Finn—

FINN

Twenty-four hours, then, just let me keep them *that* long. The world was made in six days, Father, but Heeber Finn sure won't undo it in one, will he?

FATHER LEARY *sighs, shaking his head, beaten.*

FATHER

Twenty-four hours, then. I don't want to be hard.

FINN (*smiling*)

And you're not! You're a man of reason. Here's to you, Father!

FINN *drinks.*
FATHER LEARY *picks up the broken bits and the one sign, studies them, peers at the others, starts to say something, shakes his head, moves toward the door. At the door he pauses, his back to the bartender.*

FATHER

Finn?

FINN

Yes, sir?

FATHER

If you should need me . . . don't waste time thinking on it. Give a yell.

FINN

A helluva yell, Father.

FATHER

Come early, stay late, Finn.

And the priest is gone.
FINN *exhales and strides about the bar. He wipes his brow.*

FINN

Whew, Finn, whew! I'm shaved to the bone. 'Twill take a year for my beard to grow back! Well, what's the total? Two left out

of four, but surely the most important of the whole kit. Where
was I? Men! *Boys!*

He turns to shout through the door into the back room.

Is the game done? If not, bring it out here! A free round on the
house!

VOICES

Free round! Outa the way, Men. Here we come, Finn!

The men surge out along the bar, gabbling, laughing.

THE OLD MAN

It's all in balances and weights, you get a man *so* (*Illustrates*),
and thus, and he's in the ditch before he knows the fight is over!

CASEY

Women are cats, I said, born and bred in Africa, and shipped
north to torment men in youth, middle age, and their dotage!

O'HARA

Meanness it is, keeps women alive long after a man, in his nat-
ural Christian goodness, has laid down with coins on his eyes—

FINN (*pouring*)

Drink up!

*The men drink. Each talks almost to himself. Each says, and all
only half listen, their faces rosy fire.*

KELLY

—worked in the pusstoffice selling stamps of all denominations
. . . have you ever looked at stamps, man, close? A regular
gallery of art in *one hour's* arrivals of mail from far coun-
tries . . .

*The men, drinking, look around, notice the sign, THINK, as the
talk continues, pay no attention, and go on with their blarney.*

THE OLD MAN

—in the semicircular canals I heard once on the Radio Aerrean is this liquid which dances about . . . if you can tilt a man so his semicircular canals are off center, he'll get seasick, and—

KELLY

They had a fine stamp once from Portugal, and a girl on it naked as the palm of my hand and twice as limber . . .

The talk begins to die away during all the above and on through the next speeches. One by one, the men drop out of conversation.

THE OLD MAN

Then I said to him, about fighting . . . I don't remember what I said . . . hold on . . .

CASEY

My wife has six fingers on each hand and all claws. She——
Well, that about describes . . . my . . . wife . . .

TIMULTY (*trailing off*)

Well, the bog business ain't what it was. I've said my say, I guess . . .

KELLY (*fading away*)

Then there was a stamp from . . . oh . . . but why bother . . .

O'HARA (*after a pause*)

Women are mean. Put that in your pipe and smoke it.

THE OLD MAN

Well, now . . .

TIMULTY

Yes, sir . . .

KELLY

Drink . . .

They are all suddenly uneasy and shy.

CASEY

Six fingers and claws . . .

They all look at their glasses.

FINN

Drink up, boys!

THE OLD MAN *clears his throat.* O'HARA *blows his nose. They all watch him do this, for lack of anything else to do.*

TIMULTY

Old Man, tell us that joke about Nolan on the bridge.

THE OLD MAN

I can't remember.

O'HARA *clears his throat. The men shuffle their feet. The men peer around at each other.*

O'HARA

How about some more cards?

THE OLD MAN

We was *all* losing.

TIMULTY

That's hard to do, but we did it.

Another silence.

KELLY

Well?

CASEY

Well, indeed.

They move about uneasily. They peer at each other, glance at the sign, but say nothing.

THE OLD MAN (*in a spooky voice*)

Hold on.

They all turn to look at him.

Listen.

They listen.

What do you hear?

CASEY

Nothing.

THE OLD MAN

That's it. Do you realize that this very moment and hour is the
first time in thirty years there has been silence in Heeber Finn's
pub?

FINN

Aw, now—

CASEY (*gasps*)

He's right!

KELLY

By God, he *is!*

Everyone is spooked now. The men look around.

THE OLD MAN

A lull is a strange thing to an Irishman.

KELLY (*awed*—sotto voce)

You can feel the damn thing, like a calm at sea.

They all feel it, together. FINN *is upset, but does not speak.*

THE OLD MAN (*whispering*)

Strange . . .

CASEY

Say something, Kelly.

KELLY (*blinks*)

What, for instance?

O'HARA (*whispering*)

Ah, for God's sake, man, "what for instance," *what?* he says!

KELLY

You say something, Timulty.

He checks his watch.

TIMULTY

I got to get home.

THE OLD MAN (astounded)

Home!

Timulty walks, dazed, to the door.

TIMULTY

I think so, anyway . . .

*He wanders out. All look stunned at the doors as they swing
shut.*

FINN (falsely hearty)

Here's another belt for everyone.

No answer. No enthusiasm.

KELLY

See you later . . .

FINN

Later?

And KELLY *is gone, too.*

O'HARA

I think I'll play solitaire . . .

He lays out the cards.

Ah, damn! I can see I've lost before I begin . . . So long,
boys . . .

He leaves the cards and goes.

CASEY

For all I said of the little woman, she's mine and not well . . .
I'd best go see how she does . . .

The rest follow, wordless, leaving only THE OLD MAN *and* FINN
at the bar. FINN *comes out from behind the bar in shock, almost
staggering with the blow of this great unnamed event.*

> FINN

What happened?

> THE OLD MAN (*puffs his pipe thoughtfully*)

A strange thing, for sure.

> FINN

Everybody was so happy, everybody talking, everybody bustling
about like always and then, as if the Red Death Hisself had
walked in all bones at the strike of twelve . . . hush . . . I
never heard the likes in my life! Old Man . . .

> THE OLD MAN

Hush up a bit, yourself.

THE OLD MAN *walks about the pub, sniffing, probing, squinting.
He glances now and then at the signs behind the bar and at last
stops, looking at one of the signs.* THE OLD MAN *goes behind the
bar and reaches up to handle the one sign.*

> FINN

Don't!

> THE OLD MAN

Why not?

> FINN

I hate to see something shallow touching something deep, is all!

> THE OLD MAN

Don't be so sure about your shallows and deeps, Heeber Finn!
Have you stopped to think—*this* may be the cause?

> FINN

The cause?

THE OLD MAN

Of the lull, man! Of the damn peace and quiet which suddenly befell this place? Of the becalming of this ship of yours!

FINN

"Think" did that? *THINK?*

THE OLD MAN

Think, Think, Think! Didn't you see their faces? I saw mine in the mirror, I watched it fall! I was talking along, fourteen to the dozen, when my eye spied that sign and my tongue went slower and I looked again and my lips tightened up on me and I read the *THINK!* again and the mud settled on the bottom of my brain! First thing I knew, I was "mum's the word," and so were the rest! I could see it come over them, they broke out in pale sweats! They been talking all their lives, man, and what did you do to them now?

FINN

I didn't do anything!

THE OLD MAN

Yes, you did; you asked them to think, think, think, what they was saying! That's more than enough to break a man's leg, his arm, his neck and then his back. Crippled them, you did. Called attention to their tongues and mouths. First time they had ever noticed they *had* tongues! First time they noticed they was actors, and they got stage fright! *Think* did it, man, think and nothing *but* think!

FINN (*lets out a loud cry of anguish*)

Ahhhh . . .

THE OLD MAN

Well may you groan. It's a sad day. Driving off old friends and pals. Scaring the wits out of them by showing them the marionette strings in their fingers and lips! How *could* you be so cruel, Finn?

THE OLD MAN *goes to the door.*

(*Shaken*) I *ask* myself . . . *how? How?*

He exits. FINN *is alone. He groans again and bites his knuckles, pacing the room.*

FINN

Finn, you idiot, Finn, you blathering fool! Thirty years you work to build a clientele and in one short day lop the heads and shoot the works. Lost! Finished! Done! Finn, what do you do now? Ahhh. . . .

He groans. His WIFE *comes in from the street, looks at him, looks around, moves across the pub, stops, glances over at the last sign, walks closer, peers.*

HIS WIFE

I can hardly believe my eyes.

FINN (*destroyed*)

Ah, Woman, leave me alone.

HIS WIFE (*peers*)

Does it say what I *think* it says, does it *mean* what it says? (*Spells*) D–O. . . . DO?

FINN

Leave off!

HIS WIFE (*turning*)

Why, Finn, it shows you're taking an interest. *DO!* That does mean *ACT,* and *ACT* means work, *W–O–R–K* . . . does it not?

FINN (*punished but repentent*)

It does. (*Shakes head once*)

HIS WIFE

Then you'll fix the roof today?

FINN (*bleakly*)

I'll get the tools now!

HIS WIFE

And mend the front step?

FINN (*sinking fast*)

It's good as mended!

HIS WIFE

And put a new pane of glass in our bedroom window?

FINN (*half under*)

New glass, yes!

HIS WIFE

And lay new cobblestone on the path behind?

FINN (*sunk*)

Cobblestones, glass, roof, steps, anything, everything, drive me,
sweat me, kill me with work. I deserve it. I've sinned, I want to
do penance! Make a list, Woman. Shall I paint the chairs, wax
the bar? Sew buttons on my own shirts! I will, I will, I will!

HIS WIFE (*suddenly afraid*)

Ah, God, it's all some joke!

FINN

I mean it! I'll chop turf!

HIS WIFE

You're not ill?

FINN

That all depends how you make illness out to be!

She brings him the tool kit from behind the bar.

HIS WIFE

Start with the steps, that's a love. Ah, Finn, you *are* a sweet man,
when you want to be.

FINN (*forlorn, unmoving*)

Sweet I am and glad you think so.

*She kisses him lightly on the cheek and passes toward the back
of the house.*

THE WIFE (*melodically*)
Wait for the roof till tomorrow, if you want!

She exits.

FINN (*going mad*)
Roof . . . tomorrow . . . want! Ah, ha, Finn, ah ha! Ah, ha!
There you go!

He throws the hammer through the door.

And there and there!

He throws all the tools, one by one, then the box.

Ah, Finn, there, ah ha, Finn! Look! See how it goes!

He whirls about.

What else? What, nothing? Nothing to throw, save me. And I'm
too weak to fling myself out on the stones. Ah, Finn, Finn!

*He almost weeps or maybe does, it is hard to tell with the groan-
ing. Then he sees the remaining signs. He runs and grabs them.*

All right for you, *THINK,* all right for you, *DO!* Here's the end,
the smashing end of you! You'll make fine music on the cobbles!
One, two—

He is about to throw them when the double doors open and THE
SALESMAN *peers in.*

THE SALESMAN
Ah, there, Mr. Finn, sir.

FINN
Fiend of hell, get out of the way!

THE SALESMAN
Mr. Finn . . . you sound upset, sir.

FINN *hefts the clay mottoes but does not throw them.*

FINN

Upset! Since you left this noon, it has been one plague of locusts
on another!

THE SALESMAN

The philosophical mottoes, they didn't work?

FINN

Work! They lost me the use of friends, the respect of neighbors,
the talk and the money of ancient customers, put my wife on my
shoulders along with God, the Church, and Father Leary! Hoolihan, you and your "machines" have bent and broke me. Ah! Ah!
Ah!

FINN's *hands sink to his sides. The remaining signs fall to the
floor without breaking.* FINN's *cries have become louder and
louder; he grieves at his own wake. As he shouts his last "Ah,"*
THE SALESMAN *picks up the two signs, uncertainly, whereupon
the double doors flap wide and there, with imaginary sword un-
sheathed, stands* FATHER LEARY.

FATHER

Heeber Finn, did you call!

FINN (*surprised*)

Did I? Why . . . so I *did!*

FATHER LEARY *looks around, sees and stares at* THE SALESMAN.

FATHER

Is this the one, Finn?

THE SALESMAN (*miffed*)

Is this the one *what?*

FINN

That's him, Father.

THE SALESMAN (*faintly alarmed*)

That's *who?*

FATHER (*rubbing his hands together*)

All *right,* then. All *right.*

THE SALESMAN

Is it? *What* is?

FATHER (*at the door*)

Men! Inside!

There is no instantaneous response, so FATHER LEARY *lifts his voice and strikes out a pointing hand.*

Timulty! Here! Nolan, not another step! Old Man, on the double!

He holds the door wide. THE OLD MAN *peers in.*

THE OLD MAN (*squinting right and left*)

Are they gone?

FATHER

Are what gone?

THE OLD MAN (*suspicious*)

The signs, Father.

FATHER

Ah, come on, get in!

THE OLD MAN *sidles in.* NOLAN *is behind him.*

All right, Nolan, don't clog the door.

All the men shadow-sidle in, shy and uneasy, mouthing their caps with their hands. With his army assembled, FATHER LEARY *turns to the astounded and now increasingly nervous* SALESMAN.

THE SALESMAN

What's going on?

FATHER

Well may you ask! I call your attention first to the fact that the man's wearing a suit and hat the color of burning ashes and black soot.

The men all gasp and nod in agreement.

THE SALESMAN (*controlling himself*)

Or, to put it another way, the suit was dyed this color in the factory and the rest is dirt from the roads of Eire!

FATHER LEARY *is now slowly circling the man.*

FATHER

His eyes are green—

THE SALESMAN

From my father!

FATHER

His ears pointed—

THE SALESMAN

From my mother!

THE OLD MAN

What's eatin' the priest? I——

NOLAN *gives* THE OLD MAN *a fierce elbow in the ribs which shuts him.* FATHER LEARY *plants himself before* THE SALESMAN.

FATHER

Do you mind doing one thing, man?

THE SALESMAN

What?

FATHER

Would you take off your hat?

THE SALESMAN

I *will* not!

FATHER

He won't take off his hat.

FINN

I heard him!

THE SALESMAN

The place is a tomb, I'd catch me death!

FATHER (*hitching up his trousers under his skirt*)

All right, then! Let us see your feet!

THE SALESMAN

They're right down below for you to see!

FATHER

Will you take off your shoes?

FINN

That's a *fine* idea, Father, his shoes!

THE SALESMAN

Ah, you're both daft! If I won't take off me hat I'm sure not to remove me shoes!

FATHER

He *refuses* to take off his shoes!

THE SALESMAN

What for, why?

FATHER

You know as well as I, man!

FINN

Slow down, Father, you've left us behind—

FATHER

Why, Finn, don't you see, beneath them leather clogs, he's got no toes!

THE MEN *gasp.*

It's all fused into one!

THE MEN *lean and stare.*

FINN

You mean—it's hooves he's got, instead of feet?

THE OLD MAN

Hooves?

FATHER

I didn't say that.

THE SALESMAN

No—but you infer it! I will not be cudgeled into displaying my fearful corns and bunions, for that's *all* that lies hidden there!

FATHER

So *you* say! Finn!

FINN

Yes, Father?

FATHER

Hang this bit of paper on the wall!

FINN

What is it, Father?

FATHER

Me own sign!

THE SALESMAN

Your sign? Now, that ain't right, Father. Unfair competition!

FATHER

Look at him quail!

THE SALESMAN

This ain't quailing. I'm mad!

THE OLD MAN

What's it say, Finn?

FINN (*peers at the paper*)
Sic tran–sight—glore–rye–ah—moon–day—

FATHER (*correcting him*)
Sic transit gloria mundi!

All look at THE SALESMAN.

THE OLD MAN
Look, he's gone pale!

THE SALESMAN
I ain't gone anywheres near pale! If anything, the blood pounds in me head!

THE OLD MAN
What's it mean?

FATHER
It means we're not long for this world! Post it, Finn.

FINN *hustles to nail it on the wall.*

FINN (*squinting*)
You got a teeny fine hand, Father. You can't see it six inches off!

THE OLD MAN
Sick transits, what, what?

FATHER
Gloria mundi!

THE OLD MAN
And what does it mean again, Nolan?

FATHER
Everything passes away! (*To* THE SALESMAN) Including you, sir! Get out, begone! I banish you from Heeber Finn's. I banish you from the streets of our town and the town itself!

THE SALESMAN (*backing off*)
You do indeed. It's a bunch of holy nitwits from an asylum, the town is, I'll not be back!

FATHER

That you won't.

FATHER LEARY advances upon the man, who backs to the door.

Get on! Go sell your pagan bits in Kennywell, St. Bridget's and Meynooth!

THE SALESMAN

And thanks, I will!

THE SALESMAN backs out. The double gates slam-wriggle.

FATHER

Watch out! Don't trip over your tail!

THE OLD MAN (*spying out the window*)
There he goes! He *does* walk funny!

NOLAN is at the wall, squinting at the paper.

NOLAN (*muttering*)

Sic tran–sit—

All the men look proudly at FATHER LEARY, *who turns to look at them.*

    FINN *puts a glass on the bar and fills it. He nods.* FATHER LEARY *walks to the bar and looks at the drink.*

FINN

Thank you, Father.

FATHER LEARY picks up the drink, eyes it against the light.

FATHER

It's the least I could do, for an annex of the church!

He circles his drink to take in the whole of the pub. He downs the drink.

Well, now!

He walks back to the door.

THE OLD MAN

Father! Was it wise to tell him to go sell his heathen signs to other towns?

FATHER

Ah, that's not my problem. That's the problem of the good fathers in Kennywell, St. Bridget's, and Meynooth. It's good in a way that the Devil passes by and gives us a whack and a shake and wakes us up. If I had my mind, the Fiend would make a grand tour of Ireland twice a year!

THE OLD MAN

And maybe he does, Father!

FATHER (*muses*)

Yes. Maybe he does.

FINN

Is he gone, now, Father?

FATHER LEARY *peers out.*

FATHER

The road is empty. Our trial is over. All right, then! Tonight, from seven till nine, the church is open, the booth waiting, and me inside the booth!

NOLAN

We'll be there, Father!

They hold out their drinks and drink to him.

FATHER (*surprised and pleased*)

By God, I think you will!

He exits
There is a moment of silence.

TIMULTY (*sighs*)

Well, this is a day will go down in Kilcock's history.

CASEY

It was a near thing. I almost went home to the wife . . .

TIMULTY

I almost put in for a job at the pusstoffice.

THE OLD MAN

When the Father saved us all.

TIMULTY (*musing*)

It will be known as the day the Fiend was thrown out from Heeber Finn's.

THE OLD MAN (*nose to the wall, squinting*)

Sic transit gloria mundi.

NOLAN

And what's it *mean?*

THE OLD MAN (*flaring*)

It's Latin, dimwit! That's what it means!

FINN *has walked slow to the door to look out at the church.*

FINN

A strange man.

NOLAN

The salesman?

FINN (*shakes head*)

Father Leary. Why, I ask myself, why did he tell the salesman to sell the pagan signs in Kennywell, Meynooth, and St. Bridget's? Why? *Why?*

He turns to look at the others, and at the bar. Slowly, his eyes widen, his eyebrows go up, his mouth makes a smile. Suddenly he gives a great laugh.

Ah-hah! Wife!

HIS WIFE *appears, arms over her bosom, glaring.*

Bring more chairs! A dozen!

THE WIFE

A dozen?

FINN

Make it two dozen, three, five! And tables!

HIS WIFE

Tables?

FINN

By sundown tonight refugees will be *pouring* in here from—

THE OLD MAN (*catching on*)

Kennywell?

NOLAN (*enlightened*)

Meynooth?

CASEY

And St. Bridget's!

FINN

There's no telling where from, how many, how long! It'll be a grand week end! Woman—Kathleen, sweetheart, have a drink.

She hesitates, softens, takes the drink. He gives her a buss and a pinch. FINN *raises his glass.*

Here's to not *stopping,* but going on as always and ever, with no *consideration* for one dainty moment about *thinking* and no *doing* save as how we always done. Casey, Nolan, Timulty, lend a hand!

NOLAN

It's lent!

The men rush in and out bringing tables and chairs. FINN, *in the flurry, pours a line of little glasses full. On their way in and out the men grab and swallow, hurry on.*

FINN (*sings*)

"In life, in strife,
With maid, with wife!
It's the drinkin' . . . !"

THE OLD MAN (*speaks, running*)
"Not the thinkin'!"

ALL (*sing*)

"Makes it go!"

The Curtain falls on the beehive. And . . .

THE END

The Anthem Sprinters

CHARACTERS

THE YOUNG MAN (DOUGLAS)
HEEBER FINN
THE OLD MAN
TIMULTY
DOONE
O'GAVIN
FOGARTY
NOLAN
KELLY
CASEY, PEEVEY, *and other assorted spectators, door-watchers, time-keepers and former champions of the Sprint.*

At the rise of curtain we find ourselves not so much in a real pub as in a sort of a sketch of a pub. A plank laid across two high saw-horses will do for a bar. Men are lined up, or rather clustered, at it, having a fine pantomime argument about something, shaking each other's shoulders, waving their hands, pulling their hats off and on their heads, yanking at one another's lapels, pounding their fists on the bar, and shouting silently, almost nose-to-nose. As the lights come up, so does the sound of the men, as if theatrically we were tuning in on the wildlife here. Four or five of the men are having the greatest to-do there at the rail. Two other men, down front, are Indian-wrestling each other. Two more are playing darts, hurling the feathered things through space at a target suspended far to one side. To the left a man in a bowler hat sits on a piano stool playing a tune on empty space. Though the piano is not there, we can hear it fine. It is a jolly tune. So jolly that one of the men in the argument breaks off, unable to resist, and jogs about a bit. Still another fellow somewhere in all the melee is munching on a harmonica, his eyes soulfully shut and the banshee mourn of the little machine in his mouth rising and falling in the smoke and din. An ardent fan of his stands near, aching with the melody, mouth open, watching the great musician tongue and wheeze along the contraption. In all, there are a dozen or so people littered about the scene. More can be added. Or if need be, some might be taken away and never missed.

Anyway, here we are in Heeber Finn's and FINN *himself behind the bar, singing any tune that strikes his fancy as he wipes glasses and foams up drinks, adding his own musical bit to the general commotion.*

It is a scene rather like the tumult on a pinball device when the jackpot is struck, all the lights flash, miniature guns explode, fantastic totals jump about on the scoreboard, and all the balls at once seem to rush wild down the ways.

Into this grand scene now walks our writer-hero, or for a time anyway, villain, THE YOUNG MAN. *He is not a nasty snob, he is just unfamiliar with things and, like it or not, he looks just a bit like a Tourist.*

With his entrance, some of the activity, or at least the sound of it, fades down.

THE YOUNG MAN *stands dead-center of the action and looks about, tolerantly amused. We hear a few of the cries more clearly now from some of the men arguing at the bar.*

THE MEN (*general hubbub*)

Doone!
O'Gavin!
Devil take O'Gavin!
Then Devil Take Doone! He's no Sport at all! Now—O'Gavin——

At which point THE YOUNG MAN *gathers his observations and makes his fatal comment.*

THE YOUNG MAN

Well! It sure looks like a wild night, here!

It is as if the great blade of the Guillotine had fallen. Silence chops across all. THE YOUNG MAN *is instantly sorry. Almost in midflight, the feathered dart is shot down. The piano stops. The harmonica dies in midwheeze. The dancer seems suddenly crippled. Nobody has turned yet to look at* THE YOUNG MAN. *Perhaps they are only waiting for this outlander to pack his chagrin and go away. They will give him enough time. Count to ten.* THE YOUNG MAN *looks around, looks at the door, debates heading for it, but stops.*

For one man, TIMULTY, *has broken from the mob at the bar and now slowly stalks out, not looking at* DOUGLAS, *only turning to survey him steadily after he has come full in front of him, his glass of stout in his hand.*

He drinks from the glass, eyeing DOUGLAS. DOUGLAS *fidgets. At last,* TIMULTY *speaks.*

TIMULTY

Was that said in scorn or admiration?

THE YOUNG MAN

I really can't say——

TIMULTY

There's a confusion in your mind then?

THE YOUNG MAN (*eagerly grasping this*)

Yes, that's it!

TIMULTY *turns to glance all about.*

TIMULTY

He's confused, boys!

There is a general murmur neither for nor against, in answer to this. TIMULTY *turns back.*

Are you new to Ireland, to Dublin, and to Heeber Finn's pub?

THE YOUNG MAN

Er—all *three* of those, yes!

TIMULTY (*to his friends*)

He's new to all three, boys!

There is a little more affirmative rumble now, exclamations of "Oh" and "Ah well, then" and "So that's how it is" mix with the rest. TIMULTY *views* DOUGLAS *again.*

So it's an orientation program you're in search of?

THE YOUNG MAN

That's *it!*

TIMULTY *eyes him a moment longer, then waves once, idly, to his friends.*

TIMULTY

All right, boys!

*The tumult and the shouting that had died, without the captains
and the kings departing, now instantaneously renews itself.
Darts fly. The piano sounds. The harmonica wails. The men
jump hip deep into their argumentation.*

DOUGLAS *views this, impressed, as if suddenly given to see the
vast workings of Big Ben's machinery going full blast.*

Timulty's my name.

THE YOUNG MAN

Douglas.

TIMULTY

Is it a wild night you're looking for?

THE YOUNG MAN

Well, I——

TIMULTY

You think, don't you, there *are no* Wild Nights in Ireland?

THE YOUNG MAN

I didn't say that——

TIMULTY

You think it. It shows in your eyes. Well, what would you say
if I told you you was at the eye of the hurricane! You're in the
damn earthquake, half-buried to your chin and don't know it!

THE YOUNG MAN

Am I?

TIMULTY

You are! Here at Finn's pub is the Central Betting Agency for
the greatest Sporting Event of Local Consequence!

THE YOUNG MAN

Is it?

TIMULTY

'Tis! Listen! Do you hear?

THE MEN (*yelling again*)

Two bob says you're wrong! Three bob nails you to the wall!

TIMULTY (*calling over*)

Men, what do you think of Doone?

FOGARTY

His reflex is uncanny!

THE OLD MAN

Doone hell! My money is on O'Gavin! What a Great Heart!

THE YOUNG MAN

A Sporting Event, you say?

TIMULTY

Come along! Boys, this is Mr. Douglas, from the States.

General greetings.

TIMULTY

Mr. Douglas is in—

THE YOUNG MAN

Pictures. I write screenplays for the cinema.

ALL

Fillums!

THE YOUNG MAN (*modestly*)

Films.

TIMULTY

No! It's too much!

THE OLD MAN

Are you staggered, Timulty?

TIMULTY

I am!

FOGARTY

Coincidence!

NOLAN

Beyond belief!

THE YOUNG MAN (*blinks*)

What is?

THE OLD MAN

Your occupation and our Sporting Event! They're in the same
bed!

FOGARTY

They're twins!

TIMULTY

By God now, you'll not only bet, we'll let you judge! Are you
much for sports? Do you know, for instance, such things as the
cross-country, four-forty, and like man-on-foot excursions?

THE YOUNG MAN

I've attended two Olympic Games.

THE OLD MAN (*awed*)

Not just fillums, but the World Competition!

TIMULTY

Well, now, isn't it time you knew of the special all-Irish decathlon
event which has to do with picture theatres?

THE YOUNG MAN

I—

THE OLD MAN

Shall we show him, boys?

ALL

Sure! Fine! On the way! Stand aside!

FINN

Out it is! This way! Doone, come on!

And before DOUGLAS *can protest,* bang! *they are out the door,
the pub has vanished, and they run circling through a sort of*

mist. DOONE, *who, it turns out, is the man who has been playing the invisible piano, turns last of all and, dancing around on his toes, pumping his legs like a trackman to prime himself, exits last of all, and soon catches, paces, and fronts the mob.*

FINN

Doone! Doone! There you are!

DOONE

Does an Event loom?

THE OLD MAN

It does!

DOONE (*dancing ahead*)

I'm fit!

THE OLD MAN

You are!

TIMULTY

There! We've arrived!

They pull up. THE YOUNG MAN *gazes around, still not certain what to look for.*

THE OLD MAN

Will you read *that*?

A marquee with blinking lights has come on above them.

THE YOUNG MAN

The . . . Great . . . Fine . . . Arts . . . Cinema.

TIMULTY

Don't forget "Elite." It's there. But it's burnt out.

TIMULTY *throws his cap up to hit the marquee. The missing word lights feebly and flickeringly.*

THE YOUNG MAN

The Great*ER* Fine Arts Elite Cinema Theatre.

FOGARTY

We have a name for everything, do we not?

TIMULTY

If the Arts *need* being Greater or Finer, this is where you come.

NOLAN

Ah, look at the lights move, will ya?

TIMULTY

Like the fireflies on the meadows with the sun just set.

THE OLD MAN (*nudges the writer*)

Did you *hear* him?

THE YOUNG MAN

Eh?

THE OLD MAN

Well, I mean to say, are you a writer or not? I mean, don't writers make notes of lovely things like that to put in their next book?

THE YOUNG MAN

Er . . . yes . . .

THE YOUNG MAN *takes out a pad and pencil sheepishly. Everyone leans over his shoulder to see the words go down.*

TIMULTY (*quoting himself*)

"Like the fireflies . . ."

NOLAN

". . . on the bogs . . ."

TIMULTY

"Meadows," ya dimwit! "On the meadows . . ." That's it. "With the sun . . ."

THE YOUNG MAN (*writing*)

". . . just set."

TIMULTY

There! (*Sighs*) I'm immortal.

THE OLD MAN

Enough! We are at the place of the grand sport!

THE YOUNG MAN (*dubious*)

The Greater Fine Arts Elite Cinema Theatre?

FOGARTY

Why not? Look, there's three churches in Ireland. There's them whose faith is the pubs, them whose faith is the cinemas, and then there's the Catholics.

THE OLD MAN

There's *always* a place to go.

THE YOUNG MAN

Yes, but what sport can you put in a theatre? Ping pong, basketball onstage?

TIMULTY

Doone, step forward!

DOONE, *who has been darting about on tiptoe, snorting, snuffing, dances in.*

DOONE

Doone, that's me! The Best Anthem Sprinter in Ireland!

THE YOUNG MAN

What sprinter?

DOONE (*spells with difficulty*)

A–n–t–h–e–m. Anthem. Sprinter. The fastest. (*Bobs*)

FINN

Since you've been in Dublin, have you attended the cinema?

THE YOUNG MAN

Just once, but in London last month, I saw eight films——

TIMULTY

You're fanatic, then, as are we all, through need, on this god-forsaken desert!

THE OLD MAN

In London, if you'll excuse the curse, when the fillum stopped each night, did you observe anything tending towards the peculiar?

THE YOUNG MAN (*muses*)

Hold on! You can't mean "God Save The Queen," can you?

TIMULTY

Can we, boys?

ALL

We can!

THE OLD MAN

In London, it's "God Save The Queen," here it's the National Anthem, it's all the same!

TIMULTY

Any night, every night, for tens of dreadful years, at the end of each damn fillum all over Ireland, in every cinema, as if you'd never heard the baleful tune before, the orchestra strikes up for Ireland!

THE OLD MAN (*nudges the writer*)

And what happens *then?*

THE YOUNG MAN (*muses*)

Why . . . if you're any man at all, you try to get out of the theatre in those few precious moments between the end of the film and the start of the Anthem.

TIMULTY

He's nailed it!

NOLAN

Buy the Yank a drink!

FINN (*passing bottle*)

On the house!

THE YOUNG MAN (*drinks, wipes mouth*)

After all, I was in London a month. "God Save The Queen" had
begun to pall. It's surely the same after all these years for you
and your National Anthem. (*Hastily*) No disrespect meant.

FINN

And none taken!

TIMULTY

Or *given* by any of us patriotic I.R.A. veterans, survivors of the
Troubles, lovers of country. Still, breathing the same air ten
thousand times makes the senses reel. So, as you've noted, in
that God-sent three- or four-second interval, any audience in its
right mind beats it the hell out. And the best of the crowd is—

THE YOUNG MAN

Doone. Your Anthem Sprinter.

THE OLD MAN

Smile at the man.

Everyone smiles at the American, who smiles easily back.

Now! Stand near! At this moment, not one hundred feet through
that door and down the slight declivity toward the silver screen,
seated on the aisle of the fourth row center is O'Gavin . . .

THE YOUNG MAN

. . . your *other* Anthem Sprinter.

NOLAN (*tipping his cap*)

The man's eerie.

TIMULTY (*impressed*)

O'Gavin's there, all right. He's not seen the fillum before—

THE YOUNG MAN (*looks up*)

What, Clark Gable in *It Happened One Night?*

NOLAN

Ah, that was last month. They've not got around to taking down the names.

TIMULTY

This fillum tonight is a Deanna Durbin brought back by the asking, and the time is now . . .

FINN *holds up his watch. All lean toward it.*

FINN

Ten-thirty o'clock.

TIMULTY

In five minutes the cinema will be letting the customers out in a herd . . .

THE OLD MAN

And if we should send Doone here in for a test of speed and agility . . .

DOONE (*dancing about*)

It's stripped to the buff I am!

THE OLD MAN

. . . O'Gavin would be ready to take the challenge!

THE YOUNG MAN

O'Gavin didn't go to the show just for an Anthem Sprint, did he?

THE OLD MAN

Good grief, no. He went for the Deanna Durbin songs and all, him playing the banjo and knowing music as he does. But, as I say, if he should casually note the entrance of Doone here, who would make himself conspicuous by his late arrival, O'Gavin would know what was up. They would salute each other and both sit listening to the dear music until *Finis* hove in sight.

DOONE (*doing knee-bends*)

Sure, let me at him, let me *at* him!

DOUGLAS

Do—do you have Teams?

TIMULTY

Teams! There's the Galway Runners!

FOGARTY

The Connemara Treadwells!

THE OLD MAN

The Donnegal Lightfoots!

TIMULTY

And the fastest team of all is made up of Irishmen living in London.

THE OLD MAN (*reverently*)

"The Queen's Own Evaders"!

FOGARTY

Fast, do you see, to flee from "God Save The Queen"?

All laugh, assent, pummel, gather about. FINN *searches the writer's face.*

FINN

I see the details of the sport have bewildered you. Let me nail down the rules. Fogarty?!

FOGARTY

Here!

FINN

Door-listener supreme! Nolan! Kelly!

NOLAN and KELLY

Here!

FINN

Aisle-superintendent judges! Myself—(*Shows watch*)—Time-keeper. General spectators: Casey, Peevey, and Dillon. You've met Doone. O'Gavin's in the depths, there! So much for the

participants. Now, the sports arena. (*Moves, pointing*) Much
depends on the character of the theatre.

THE YOUNG MAN

The character?

THE OLD MAN (*hustling along*)

Here's the exits, ya see? And inside—(*Opens a door, points*)
—the lobby . . .

FINN (*cuts in*)

Now, there be some liberal free-thinking theatres with grand
aisles, grand lobbies, grand exits, and even grander, more spa-
cious latrines . . .

NOLAN (*cutting in*)

Some with so much porcelain, the echoes alone put you in
shock . . .

TIMULTY (*cutting in*)

And then again there's the parsimonious mousetrap cinemas
with aisles that squeeze the breath from you, seats that knock
your knees, and doors best sidled out of on your way to the
men's lounge in the sweet-shop across the alley.

THE OLD MAN

Each theatre is carefully assessed before, during, and after a
Sprint. A runner is judged by whether he had to fight through
men and women en masse, mostly men, women with shopping
bags which is terrible, or worst still, children at the flypaper mati-
nees.

NOLAN (*illustrating*)

The temptation with children of course is lay into them as you'd
harvest hay, tossing them in windrows to left and right.

THE OLD MAN

So we've stopped that. Now it's nights only here at the ideal
cinema of them all.

THE YOUNG MAN

Ideal? Why?

KELLY (*displays tape measure*)
Its aisles, do you see, are neither too wide nor too narrow.

He and THE OLD MAN *pace off by the exit door. They illustrate with the tape.*

Its exits are well placed.

THE OLD MAN (*tests door*)
The door hinges oiled.

They open the door and point in. THE YOUNG MAN *peers.*

TIMULTY
Its crowds, do you see? are a proper mixture of sporting bloods and folks who mind enough to leap aside should a Sprinter, squandering his energy, come dashing up the way.

THE YOUNG MAN (*suddenly thoughtful*)
Do you . . . handicap your runners?

FINN
We do!

THE OLD MAN
Some nights, we put a summer coat on one, a winter coat on another of the racers.

TIMULTY
Or seat one chap in the fifth row, while the other takes the third.

FINN
And if a man turns terrible feverish swift, we add the sweetest known burden of all—

THE YOUNG MAN
Drink?

ALL
Ah . . . ah . . . ah . . .

All laugh, mumble, move in to clap and pat the dear, knowledge-able boy.

THE OLD MAN

What else! Nolan! Run this in! Make O'Gavin take two swigs, big ones! (*Aside*) He's a *two-handicap* man.

NOLAN *runs through the door.*

NOLAN

Two it is!

TIMULTY

While Doone here has already made his weight at Heeber Finn's.

DOONE (*drinking from the bottle*)

Even all!

KELLY

Go on, Doone. Let our money be a light burden on you. Let's see you burst out that exit, five minutes from now, victorious and first.

FINN

Doone! Inside!

DOONE *shakes hands all around. He waves to everyone as if going on a long voyage, opens the door. Sweet music flushes out about him—he basks in it a moment, then plunges through into darkness, gone. At which point* NOLAN *bursts back out.*

NOLAN (*waves flask*)

O'Gavin's handicapped!

THE OLD MAN

Fine! Kelly, now, go check the contestants, be sure they sit opposite each other in the fourth row, caps on, coats half buttoned, scarves properly furled.

KELLY (*running*)

It's already done!

KELLY *vanishes back through in a surge of music of great romance.*

FINN (*checking his watch*)

In two more minutes—

THE YOUNG MAN (*innocently*)

Post Time?

TIMULTY (*with admiring affection*)

You're a dear lad.

KELLY (*bursting through door*)

All set! They're ready!

FOGARTY (*listening at the door*)

'Tis almost over, you can tell, toward the end of any fillum, the music has a way of getting out of hand!

He opens the door wide and nods in. Sure enough, the music is in full heat now, surging all over the place. All listen and nod, eyes closed.

TIMULTY

Full orchestra and chorus behind the singing maid. I must come tomorrow for the entirety.

FINN (*entranced*)

What's the tune?

THE OLD MAN

Ah, off with the tune! Lay the bets!

FINN (*recovering*)

Right! Who's for Doone, who O'Gavin?

ALL (*hustling about, waving money and paper*)

Doone! A shilling for O'Gavin. Doone! Two says it's Doone! Four on O'Gavin!

THE YOUNG MAN (*holding out money*)

O'Gavin.

FINN (*shocked*)

Without having *seen* him?

THE YOUNG MAN (*whispers*)

A dark horse.

TIMULTY

A brave choice. Kelly, Nolan, inside as aisle judges. Watch sharp there's no jumping the *Finis*.

In go KELLY *and* NOLAN, *happy as boys.*

FINN

Make an aisle now. Yank, you over here with me!

All rush to form a double line, one on either side of the exit.

TIMULTY

Fogarty, lay your ear to the door!

FOGARTY (*does so*)

The damn music is extra loud!

THE OLD MAN (sotto voce *to* THE YOUNG MAN)

It will be over soon. Whoever's to die is dying this moment!

FOGARTY

Louder still! There!

He holds one door half wide. The last single chord of music blasts out.

FINN

The grand ta-ta! By God!

THE YOUNG MAN (*a quiet exclamation*)

They're *off!*

FINN

Stand aside! Clear the door!

FOGARTY (*listens*)

Here they come!

FINN

Listen to their feet!

THE OLD MAN

Like thunder it is!

We hear the feet rushing.

FINN

Come on, O'Gavin!

TIMULTY

Doone! Doone!

ALL

Doone! O'Gavin! Doone! O'Gavin!

The doors burst wide. DOONE, *breathless, plunges out alone.*

The winner!

DOONE (*surprised*)

By God, so I *am!*

FINN

'Tenshun! The National Anthem!

He holds the door wide. The men whip off their caps. The Anthem speeds swiftly to its end.

THE YOUNG MAN (*puzzled*)

That was quick. Did they leave something out?

FINN

What *didn't* they!!

THE OLD MAN

Over the years, by some miracle or other, the Anthem has got shorter and shorter.

DOONE

Where's my competition?

All suddenly realize DOONE *stands alone, blinking back into the cinema dark, from which* NOLAN *and* KELLY *emerge, bewildered.*

THE OLD MAN

Jesus, you're right! Where's O'Gavin!

NOLAN

The idiot didn't run out the wrong exit, did he?

DOONE (*calling into the dark*)

O'Gavin!?

KELLY

Could he've sprinted into the Men's?

FINN

Now what would he do there?

THE OLD MAN (*snorts*)

There's a son of ignorant Ireland for you! *O'Gavin!*

FOGARTY

Good grief, maybe coming up the aisle he had a heart attack
and is lying there in the dark gasping his—

ALL

That's *it!*

The men riot through the door, THE YOUNG MAN *last.*

NOLAN

Maybe he broke his leg.

KELLY

Did you bring the gun?

THE OLD MAN

Ah, off with the gun! O'Gavin? Dear lad? How *is* it?

*They mob around down, perhaps to the first row of the theatre,
where they all peer at one man seated alone.*

NOLAN

O'Gavin!

FINN

You haven't *moved!*

THE OLD MAN
Why are you *sittin'* there?

FINN
What's that on his cheek?

FOGARTY (*bends close, peers*)
A teardrop! A tear!

O'GAVIN (*moans*)
Ah, God!

FINN
O'Gavin, are ya sick?

They all bend close.

O'GAVIN
Ah, God . . .

He rises slowly and turns, brushing a tear from his eye. He shakes his head beatifically, eyes shut.

She has the voice of an angel.

THE YOUNG MAN
Angel?

O'GAVIN (*nods back at the stage*)
That one up there, on the silver screen.

They all turn to stare at a silver screen that has come down behind them, where Finn's pub once was.

THE YOUNG MAN
Deanna Durbin, does he mean?

O'GAVIN (*blowing his nose*)
The dear dead voice of my grandmother—

TIMULTY

Your grandma's behind!

THE YOUNG MAN (*peering at the screen*)

Her singing? Just *that* made him forget to run?

O'GAVIN

Just! *Just!* It would be sacrilege to bound from a cinema after
a recital such as that just heard! Might as well throw bombs at
a wedding or—

TIMULTY

You could've at least *warned* us it was No Contest.

O'GAVIN

How? It crept over me in a divine sickness. That last bit she
sang. "The Lovely Isle of Innisfree," was it not, Doone?

FOGARTY

What *else* did she sing?

THE OLD MAN (*exasperated*)

What *else?* He's just lost some of you a day's wages and you
ask what else she sang!

O'GAVIN

Sure, it's money that runs the world. But it is music which holds
down the friction.

PHIL (*a voice from the back of the theatre*)

Hey! What's going on down there!

TIMULTY (*aside to the Yank*)

It's the cinema projectionist—!

THE OLD MAN

Hello, Phil, darling! It's only the Team!

FINN

We've a bit of a problem here, Phil, in ethics, not to say es-
thetics.

THE OLD MAN (*smiling his grandest*)
Yes, now, we wonder—could you run the Anthem over?

PHIL'S VOICE
Run it *over?!*

There is a rumble of protests from the winners, approval from the losers.

O'GAVIN
A *lovely* idea!

TIMULTY
It *is* not! Doone won fair and square!

THE OLD MAN
An Act of God incapacitated O'Gavin!

KELLY
A tenth-run flicker from the year nineteen hundred and thirty-seven caught him by the short hairs, you mean!

FOGARTY
We've never run a sprint over before——

O'GAVIN (*sweetly*)
Phil, dear boy, is the *last* reel of the Deanna Durbin fillum still there?

PHIL'S VOICE
It ain't in the Ladies'.

O'GAVIN
What a wit the boy has. Now, Phil, do you think you could just thread the singing girl back through the infernal machine there and give us the *Finis* again?

PHIL
Is *that* what you *all* want?

There is a hard moment of indecision.

FOGARTY (*tempted*)

Including, of course, all of the song "The Lovely Isle of Innisfree"?

PHIL

The whole damn island, sure!

Everybody beams. This has hit them where they live.

THE OLD MAN

Done! Places, everyone!

DOONE *and* O'GAVIN *race to sit down.*

THE YOUNG MAN

Hold on! There's no audience. Without them, there're no obstacles, no real contest.

FINN (*scowls, thinks*)

Why, let's *all* of us be the audience!

ALL (*flinging themselves into seats*)

Grand! Fine! Wonderful!

THE YOUNG MAN *is left alone, looking at his friends.*

THE YOUNG MAN

I beg pardon.

THE OLD MAN (*seated*)

Yes, lad?

THE YOUNG MAN

There's no one outside by the exit, to judge who wins.

Everyone is shocked to hear this. They look around.

TIMULTY

Then, Yank, would you mind doing us the service?

THE YOUNG MAN *nods, backs off, then turns and runs back out to the exit door, onstage.*

PHIL'S VOICE

Are ya clods down there ready?

THE OLD MAN (*turning*)

If Deanna Durbin and the Anthem is!

PHIL'S VOICE

Here goes!

The lights go out. The music surges. A voice sings. By the exit door, THE YOUNG MAN *tenses, waiting, checking his watch. He holds the door half open, listening.*

THE YOUNG MAN

Forty seconds . . . thirty . . . ten seconds . . . there's the Finale . . . ! They're—*Off!*

He flings himself back as if afraid a flood of men will mob out over him. We hear the grand Ta-Ta of cymbals, drums, brass. Then—silence.

THE YOUNG MAN *opens the door wide and peers into the dark, then stiffens to attention as*

The National Anthem plays. Even shorter this time, at double-quick speed.

When it is over, THE YOUNG MAN *steps in and peers down at the long row where the "audience" and the two competitors are seated. They all stand and look back and up at the projection room.*

Tears are streaming from their eyes. They are dabbing their cheeks.

THE OLD MAN (*calls*)

Phil, darling . . . ?

FINN

. . . once more?

They all sit down. Only TIMULTY *remains standing, eyes wet. He gestures.*

148 THE ANTHEM SPRINTERSTHE ANTHEM SPRINTERS

TIMULTY

And this time . . . *without* the Anthem?

Blackout.

Music. A swift Irish reel, with blended overtones of the lilting "Innisfree," old Deanna Durbin songs, and at the very last, the Anthem, in its most truncated form.

The real *audience can, if it wishes, run for the exits, now, for our Play has come to*

THE END

The Queen's Own Evaders,

an Afterword *by Ray Bradbury*

I had never wanted to go to Ireland in my life.

Yet here was John Huston on the telephone asking me to his hotel for a drink. Later that afternoon, drinks in hand, Huston eyed me carefully and said, "How would you like to live in Ireland and write *Moby Dick* for the screen?"

And suddenly we were off after the White Whale; myself, the wife, and two daughters.

It took me seven months to track, catch, and throw the Whale flukes out.

From October to April I lived in a country where I did not want to be.

I thought that I saw nothing, heard nothing, felt nothing of Ireland. The Church was deplorable. The weather was dreadful. The poverty was inadmissible. I would have none of it. Besides, there was this Big Fish . . .

I did not count on my subconscious tripping me up. In the middle of all the threadbare dampness, while trying to beach Leviathan with my typewriter, my antennae were noticing the people. Not that my wide-awake self, conscious and afoot, did not notice them, like and admire and have some for friends, and see them often, no. But the overall thing, pervasive, was the poorness and the rain and feeling sorry for myself in a sorry land.

With the Beast rendered down into oil and delivered to the cameras, I fled Ireland, positive I had learned naught save how to dread storms, fogs, and the penny-beggar streets of Dublin and Kilcock.

But the subliminal eye is shrewd. While I lamented my hard work and my inability, every other day, to feel as much like Herman Melville as I wished, my interior self kept alert, snuffed deep, listened long, watched close, and filed Ireland and its people for other times when I might relax and let them teem forth to my own surprise.

151

I came home via Sicily and Italy where I had baked myself free of the Irish winter, assuring one and all, "I'll write nothing ever about the Connemora Lightfoots and the Donnybrook Gazelles."

I should have remembered my experience with Mexico, many years before, where I had encountered not rain and poverty, but sun and poverty, and come away panicked by a weather of mortality and the terrible sweet smell when the Mexicans exhaled death. I had at last written some fine nightmares out of that.

Even so, I insisted, Eire was dead, the wake over, her people would never haunt me.

Several years passed.

Then one rainy afternoon Mike (whose real name is Nick), the taxi-driver, came to sit just out of sight in my mind. He nudged me gently and dared to remind me of our journeys together across the bogs, along the Liffey, and him talking and wheeling his old iron car slow through the mist night after night, driving me home to the Royal Hibernian Hotel, the one man I knew best in all the wild green country, from dozens of scores of Dark Journeys.

"Tell the truth about me," Mike said. "Just put it down the way it was."

And suddenly I had a short story and a play. And the story is true and the play is true. It happened like that. It could have happened no other way.

Well, the story we understand, but why, after all these years, did I turn to the stage?

It was not a turn, but a return.

I acted on the amateur stage, and radio, as a boy. I wrote plays as a young man. These plays, unproduced, were so bad that I promised myself never to write again for the stage until late in life, after I'd learned to write all the other ways first and best. Simultaneously, I gave up acting because I dreaded the competitive politics actors must play in order to work. Besides: the short story, the novel, called. I answered. I plunged into writing. Years passed. I went to hundreds of plays. I loved them. I read hundreds of plays. I loved them. But still I held off from ever writing Act I, Scene I, again. Then came *Moby Dick,* a while to brood over it, and suddenly here was Mike, my taxi-driver, rummaging my soul, lifting up titbits of adventure from a few years before near the Hill of Tara or inland at the autumn changing of leaves in Killeshandra. My old love of the theater with a final shove pushed me over.

One other thing jolted me back toward the stage. In the last five years I have borrowed or bought a good many European and American Idea Plays to read; I have watched the Absurd and the More-Than-Absurd Theatre. In the aggregate I could not help but judge the plays as frail exercises, more often than not half-witted, but above all lacking in the prime requisites of imagination and ability.

It is only fair, given this flat opinion, I should now put my own head on the chopping-block. You may, if you wish, be my executioners.

This is not so unusual. Literary history is filled with writers who, rightly or wrongly, felt they could tidy up, improve upon, or revolutionize a given field. So, many of us plunge forward where angels leave no dustprint.

Having dared once, exuberant, I dared again. When Mike vaulted from my machine, others unbidden followed.

And the more that swarmed, the more jostled to fill the spaces.

I suddenly saw that I knew more of the minglings and commotions of the Irish than I could disentangle in a month or a year of writing and unraveling them forth. Inadvertently, I found myself blessing the secret mind, and winnowing a vast interior post-office, calling nights, towns, weathers, beasts, bicycles, churches, cinemas, and ritual marches and flights by name.

Mike had started me at an amble; I broke into a trot which was before long a Full Sprint pacing my dear friends, the Queen's Own Evaders.

The stories, the plays, were born in a yelping litter. I had but to get out of their way.

Now done, and busy with other plays about science-fiction machineries which will spin their cogs in yet another book—do I have an after-the-fact theory to fit play-writing?

Yes.

For only after, can one nail down, examine, explain.

To try to know beforehand is to freeze and kill.

Self-consciousness is the enemy of all art, be it acting, writing, painting, or living itself, which is the greatest art of all.

Here's how my theory goes. We writers are up to the following:

We build tensions toward laughter, then give permission, and laughter comes.

We build tensions toward sorrow, and at last say cry, and hope to see our audience in tears.

We build tensions toward violence, light the fuse, and run.

We build the strange tensions of love, where so many of the other tensions mix to be modified and transcended, and allow that fruition in the mind of the audience.

We build tensions, especially today, toward sickness and then, if we are good enough, talented enough, observant enough, allow our audiences to be sick.

Each tension seeks its own proper end, release, and relaxation.

No tension, it follows, aesthetically as well as practically, must be built which remains unreleased. Without this, any art ends incomplete, halfway to its goal. And in real life, as we know, the failure to relax a particular tension can lead to madness.

There are seeming exceptions to this, in which novels or plays end at the height of tension, but the release is implied. The audience is asked to go forth into the world and explode an idea. The final action is passed on from creator to reader-viewer whose job it is to finish off the laughter, the tears, the violence, the sexuality, or the sickness.

Not to know this is not to know the essence of creativity, which, at heart, is the essence of man's being.

If I were to advise new writers, if I were to advise the new writer in myself, going into the theatre of the Absurd, the almost-Absurd, the theatre of Ideas, the any-kind-of-theatre-at-all, I would advise like this:

Tell me no pointless jokes.

I will laugh at your refusal to allow me laughter.

Build me no tension toward tears and refuse me my lamentations.

I will go find me better wailing walls.

Do not clench my fists for me and hide the target.

I might strike you, instead.

Above all, sicken me not unless you show me the way to the ship's rail.

For, please understand, if you poison me, I must be sick. It seems to me that many people writing the sick film, the sick novel, the sick play, have forgotten that poison can destroy minds even as it can destroy flesh. Most poison bottles have emetic recipes stamped on the labels. Through neglect, ignorance, or inability, the new intellectual Borgias cram hairballs down our throats and refuse us the convulsion that could make us well. They have forgotten, if they ever knew, the ancient knowledge that only by being truly sick can one regain health. Even beasts know when it is good and proper to throw up. Teach me how to be sick then, in the right time and place, so that I may again walk in the fields and with the wise and smiling dogs know enough to chew sweet grass.

The art aesthetic is all encompassing, there is room in it for every horror, every delight, if the tensions representing these are carried to their furthest perimeters and released in action. I ask for no happy endings. I ask only for proper endings based on proper assessments of energy contained and given detonation.

Given all this, what are we to make of a book mainly composed of Irish comedies?

Well, the means whereby men "make do" with the world,

which is more often than not by their wit and humor, is the good
stuff of serious thought. We think long and much on the universe
and the ways of God and man toward man, and then cry into
our inkwells to service tragedies, or throw our heads way back
and give one hell of a yell of laughter.

This time out, given poverty, given bicycle collisions in fogs
that might turn deadly serious, given rank prejudice and raw
bias, given suicidal cold and insufficient means against such cold,
given Ireland that is, and all its priest-ridden and sleet-worn
souls, I have chosen to lift my head from my hands, I have
chosen not to weep but to laugh with them as they themselves
must laugh, in order to survive, in the pubs, and on the roads
of a lost and much-overpraised bog.

To take the plays more or less in the order of their veracity
to life and my experience in Ireland, THE FIRST NIGHT OF
LENT, as I have already noted, is a true portrayal of my ad-
ventures with Mike, the lone taxi-driver of Kilcock.

THE GREAT COLLISION OF MONDAY LAST is based
a bit more roughly on Truth, with a sidewise look at fancy and a
backward glance at the lie which, once gone over, cannot be
treaded again, for now it is booby-trapped. The fact is, collisions
occur all the time in Ireland between hell-bent sinner bicyclists,
with dread results. From the echoes of multiple collisions I
harkened for further reverberations which became the play.

A CLEAR VIEW OF AN IRISH MIST can best be approached thiswise:

If Tintoretto, Michelangelo, Titian and others invented the
wide-screen frozen cinema of the Renaissance, it was the Irish
first came full-blown with the Hi-Fi and the Long-Play Stereo.

Just open the doors of any pub, stand out of the blast, and
you'll know what I mean.

I woke one night in Dublin, half-panicked by something,
shook my wife and cried, I think, "The Troubles! They're on
again!" or perhaps "There's a riot downstairs!"

"No such thing," my wife murmured, rolling over. "There

was a dance up the street. It's just letting out." Or perhaps she protested, falling into a snooze, "They've just shut the pubs . . ."

No matter. A great river of Irish swept by below, all "tweeter," all "woofer," and playing on forever.

The flood took the better part of an hour to die away and empty into the Liffey; for little side-flurries swept into storefronts or whirlpooled at streetcorners with fearful arguments and ardent proclamations. Poets were striking blows for freedom, actors were pounding Yeats into the earth just to yank him out again. If women or girls were present they were stormed to silence by the concussions.

In sum, if Guinness is the national stout, conversation is the royal republican wine, liberally manufactured and sold everywhere men so much as bump elbows in passing.

Irishmen inhale but never exhale: they *talk*.

And they surely regret the lost time it takes to draw breath, for during that split second some idiot with full lungs might dart in to seize the arguments and not give them back save by main force.

Given this overall and inescapable truth, I have fancied forth A CLEAR VIEW OF AN IRISH MIST to show what might happen to the National LP and the dear Hi-Fi should an irrational beast dare them to THINK.

Which leaves us at last with the Anthem Sprinters themselves.

Squashed betwixt wet sky and damp earth, sex has little place to lie down in anywhere from Dublin to Galway. Women, strange creatures that they be, hesitate but a moment when offered a choice between a sodden tromp for love in the flooded fields or the dry cinema where one can squeeze out one's passions as well as can be under the circumstances by knocking knees, clubbing feet and squirming elbows. If the girl did not make this choice, the Church would make it for her. The growing and tumescent lad then has but two ports to put in at, the pub and the cinema. Both places overflow in all towns any night.

But the Church and State, synonymous, lurk everywhere.

The pubs close too early for Reason to have been completely defeated.

The American "fillums," which make clerical collars to jump up and down in apprehension, are censored.

And, Worst, at the end of each show, the damn Anthem is played.

It was while in Dublin, nightly attending old Wally Beery movies to get in out of the cold, I first noticed that my wife and I, like the rest, were on our feet and half up the aisle before FINIS hit the screen.

This observation put me within a hair of forming teams and scoring champs for their ability to make the MEN'S split seconds ahead of the infernal national ditty.

These plays have taught me much, but mostly about myself. I hope never, as a result, to doubt my subconscious again. I hope always to stay alert, to educate myself. But lacking this, in future I will turn back to my secret mind to see what it has observed at a time when I thought I was sitting this one out.

These then are a blind man's plays, suddenly seen. I am grateful that part of me paid attention and saved coins when I could have sworn I was poverty-stricken.

In addition, one can only hope that these plays have been taken in small doses, one at a time. One-act plays, short stories, shots of the best Irish whiskey, all should be savored separate and apart. Too, if one should sit down to read all these plays in one night, one would discover certain encounters or facts in one play not connecting up with encounters or facts in another. This results from all the plays being written separately, with no thought being given to plays future or plays past. The result is a series of one-acts meant to be done separately and read in the same fashion. Though, of course, with a few deletions and additions, the entirety could be staged of an evening. I have chosen, however, to let the plays stand as they are, separate and apart, for they are more enjoyable as creative units, and I insist you must look on them as such; that is my prerogative.

Call all of what you have read in this book mere frivolous calligraphy if you wish. But here, I believe, we find ways of making do with squalls of weather, melancholy drizzles of church rhetoric, the improbability if not the impossibility of sex, the inevitability of death, and the boring ritual of the same old pomp-and-drum corp washing, hanging out, and taking in the same tired old national linen.

The church has put her on her knees, the weather drowned, and politics all but buried her, but Ireland, dear God, with vim and gusto, still sprints for that far EXIT.

And, do you know? I think she'll make it.

Ray Bradbury
July 31st, 1962